Modern Times

Modern Times

Temporality in Art and Politics

JACQUES RANCIÈRE

TRANSLATED BY
GREGORY ELLIOTT

VERSO
London • New York

This English-language edition first published by Verso 2022
Translation © Gregory Elliott 2021
This expanded edition first published as *Les temps modernes: Art, temps, politique*
© La Fabrique 2018

13 5 7 9 10 8 6 4 2

Verso
UK: 6 Meard Street, London W1F 0EG
US: 20 Jay Street, Suite 1010, Brooklyn, NY 11201
versobooks.com

Verso is the imprint of New Left Books
9781839763236
ISBN-13: 978-1-83976-319-9
ISBN-13: 978-1-83976-322-9 (UK EBK)
ISBN-13: 978-1-83976-323-6 (US EBK)

British Library Cataloguing in Publication Data
A catalogue record for this book is available from the British Library

Library of Congress Control Number: 2021948555

Typeset in Fournier by MJ&N Gavan, Truro, Cornwall
Printed and bound by CPI Group (UK) Ltd, Croydon CR0 4YY

CONTENTS

PREFACE TO THE FRENCH EDITION

Some explanation is doubtless required when one has the audacity to borrow the title of a famous film and a famous journal. The simplest, and most precise, consists in stating that, appearances to the contrary notwithstanding, the title in French – *Les temps modernes* – is not the same. The use of the plural accounts for the difference. It is normally a figure of speech to convey the modern age or condition. Sartre followed this usage when introducing the first issue of *Temps modernes*. There he invokes the writer's total commitment in their 'age', conceived as a totality, a 'meaningful synthesis'.[1] Thus his text declines 'the time' or 'the age' in the singular. The same is not true here. This book involves neither a diagnosis of modernity, nor an appeal to embrace the time. Instead, it ponders the montage of time that makes it possible to issue such an appeal or

---

1 Jean-Paul Sartre, *Les Temps modernes* 1 (October 1945), p. 20.

advance a diagnosis. The reference to Charlie Chaplin's film helps us to formulate the problem. Its dramaturgy is based on an obvious clash between two temporalities: the swaying movement of the tramp who takes his time and the inexorable rhythm of the machine that forces him into the compulsive gesture of someone who cannot stop tightening nuts and bolts, and who hallucinates that they are everywhere. But Chaplin's contemporaries had already asked themselves this question: are the automatic character of the insouciant tramp's gestures and the machine's infernal rhythms really antithetical? In fact, prior to embodying denunciation of the industrial age in the name of some dubious nostalgia for romantic bohemia, Chaplin had embodied the precise opposite. The Soviet artistic avant-garde made him a fellow of Lenin and Edison: a man whose gestures were perfectly adapted to the punctuality of the machine about to sweep away the detritus of the old world. It is true that adherents of this avant-garde had themselves been treated as gentle dreamers by those who deemed themselves the real avant-garde: the leaders of the Soviet Communist Party, who were not concerned with the aesthetic synchronization of machines and gestures, but looked to them to accumulate the wealth that would form the basis of a future communism, at the cost of protracted effort and unremitting discipline.

Opposed movements, opposed modernities, opposed avant-gardes: the conflict over what modern times are has only intensified. In truth, it goes back a long way. In 1847, the *Communist Manifesto* saluted the historical work of a bourgeoisie that had prepared the socialist future by liquidating antiquated feudal structures and ideologies. Was Marx aware that he was adopting the thesis of counter-revolutionaries denouncing the fatal rise of modern individualism for the cause of a future collectivist revolution? In all events, there is no doubt that, a few years earlier, he had proposed a quite different analysis of the relations between past, present and future: if the revolution was going to occur in Germany, he had argued, it was on account of German retardation; more precisely, because of the discrepancy between the lead taken by German philosophy and the backwardness of the country's feudal and bureaucratic structures. In the same years, in the United States, Emerson also diagnosed a discrepancy, summoning the future poet who would know how to bridge the gap between the country's material development and its spiritual infirmity. And it was precisely in this lag, in the fact that modern America was still in pre-Homeric times when it came to culture, that he perceived the possibility of such a poet emerging. We know how Walt Whitman would realize his wish by donning the apparel of a new Homer, and providing future revolutionaries with the model of a poetry drawn from the prose of everyday life. Later on, his compatriots Loie Fuller and Isadora Duncan arrived to play the maenads of the electric age or to revive the movements depicted on ancient Greek vases for a dance of the future. In their wake, Dziga Vertov tasked three ballerinas with synthesizing the movements of the communist working day on screen, only the following year to see his colleague and enemy Eisenstein oppose to his modern symphony of machines a mythological bull ceremony, which to him was much more apt as a symbol of the collective dynamism of the new times.

We could extend the list of the contradictions and paradoxes we encounter in any discourse on modernity. But for now it is enough to confirm the following: there is no one modern times, only a plurality of them, of frequently different, and sometimes contradictory, ways of thinking the time of modern politics or modern art in terms of progress, regression, repetition, arrest or overlapping times; different or contradictory ways of organizing the temporalities of the arts of movement – their continuities, breaks, forms of splicing and resumption – to create works responding to present conditions and future exigencies. This interlacing, and these clashes of temporalities, were what I chose to talk about to endow with some coherence a series of lectures given at the instigation of friends in various countries of the former Yugoslavia. In Skopje, I queried the way in which the time of politics is narrated and sought, to rethink it not as a line stretching between a past and a future, but as a conflict over the distribution of life forms. In Novi Sad, on the basis of this conflict, I tried to redefine what is to be understood by the ambiguous term 'artistic modernity'. In Zagreb and Sarajevo, I analysed the way that cinema, in order to speak of its time, combined the heterogeneous temporalities of narrative, performance and myth. A proposal was then made to me by the Multimedijalni Institut of Zagreb to publish a collection comprising these three talks. It seemed to me perfectly in keeping to add a talk on 'The Moment of Dance' given elsewhere, but whose themes and issues chimed so well with theirs. Two of the talks were initially written in English, while the other two went through French and English versions. The original edition of this book was published in English in 2017 in Zagreb, under the title *Modern Times: Essays on Temporality in Art and Politics*. Eric Hazan then expressed a desire to publish a French version. Translating texts composed in a foreign language into one's mother tongue is a tolerable exercise only on condition of being an unfaithful translator. I have therefore not sought simply to furnish a French equivalent of the English version, but have taken the opportunity to rewrite passages and make various changes. Thus, what francophone readers have in their hands is a book that is faithful to its original, but new in its formulation. All those who made the existence of both editions possible will find my warmest thanks in the Acknowledgements.

Paris, February 2018

ACKNOWLEDGEMENTS

The impetus for this book comes from lecture tours kindly organized for me in various countries of the former Yugoslavia by Ivana Momčilović, the director of Jugoslavija Books. I would like to thank her, along with those who helped her in this task – especially Petar Milat and Leonardo Kovačević of Zagreb's Multimedijalni Institut (MaMa), as well as Zdravko Vulin and Aleksandar Oparnica of the Student Cultural Centre of Novi Sad (SKCNS).

The original version of 'Time, Narrative, Politics' dates from May 2014, when it was delivered at Skopje's Institute of Social Sciences and Humanities at the invitation of Katerina Kolozova. An English translation by Drew Burk was published in 2015 in the eleventh issue of the journal *Identities*. The present text is based on a new English version written by the author for a talk given in January

2015 at the CalArts Institute of Los Angeles at the invitation of Martin Plot.

'Modernity Revisited' was given in May 2014 in Novi Sad at the invitation of the SKCNS.

'The Moment of Dance' was written for the colloquium on 'Dance in/and Theory' organized in April 2014 at Brown University (Providence) by Michelle Clayton and Zachary Sng.

'Cinematic Moments' was given in October 2015 at the MaMa (Zagreb) and the University of Sarajevo at the invitation of Tijana Okic. An initial version was presented in June 2015 at the Cinema Ritrovato festival in Bologna.

All these texts were reworked several times for their original publication in English, as indeed they have been for the French edition.

I am grateful to Petar Milat for the idea, and for the beautiful typographical production of the original English edition. Finally, I would like to thank Eric Hazan, who had the idea of the French edition, as well as Stella Magliani-Belkacem and Jean Morisot of Editions La Fabrique for their kind attention to my work.

1
TIME, NARRATIVE, POLITICS

'There has been history, but there is no longer any.' Such are the terms in which Marx sums up Proudhon's method, which (according to him) transforms economic categories into eternal ideas. Proudhon sought to derive principles of fair exchange between agents in the economic process from a timeless justice. Against this, Marx pitted a justice that was the product of history, a goal to be attained by the historical development of the relations of production and exchange. Our age would appear to have deflected this criticism back onto him. It teaches us that the History which Marx counter-posed to the naive worship of eternal justice is itself a *story*: the fiction of a temporal development guided by a future end, the grand narrative of a wrong inflicted and justice promised to a universal victim. We are invited to accept today that that history no longer exists, that the reality of the time we live in has brought its age to a close.

I shall return to the conclusions our contemporaries think they can draw from what they have called the end of grand narratives. I should first of all like to stress the common manner in which Marx's critique and the critique of Marxism dramatize time: as a principle of reality (what we think in atemporal categories is merely perceived by us from a point located in time); as a principle of rationality (what we have before us as raw reality is intelligible only when articulated in a temporal series of causes and effects); and as an actor rendering a certain justice. For some, it will put an end to putatively objective realities and professedly eternal categories. For others, it will do away with the illusory promises that people have endeavoured to get time to keep. I shall come back to what this dramaturgy involves and what it represses. But first I must note a preliminary point. This dramaturgy, common to the invocation of a science of history and to its condemnation, refers to a certain type of rationality: fictional rationality.

I have had various occasions to say: fiction is not the invention of imaginary beings. In the first instance, it is a structure of rationality. It is the construction of a framework within which subjects, things and situations are seen as belonging to a common world, while events can be identified and linked in terms of coexistence, succession and causal linkage. Fiction is required whenever a certain sense of reality needs to be produced. That is why political action, social science and journalistic practice employ fictions, just like novelists or filmmakers. And this fictional rationality invariably boils down to a basic kernel, which is a certain justice of time: a causal order where events come after one another and situations are reversed; a process of unveiling in which subjects become conscious of this sequence and experience these reversals. This matrix structure, connecting events that succeed one another, situations that are turned upside down, and subjects who experience their effect and acquire knowledge of them, goes back a long way. In the West, it was established by Aristotle's *Poetics*. But it still enables us to understand and query the common way in which the science of history, and the discourse that claims it has expired, think the relationship between time and justice.

The fact is that, since the fall of the Soviet Empire, the dominant descriptions of the present time have employed a crudely positivistic notion of time. Under various rubrics — the end of utopia, the end of grand narratives and so forth — and in more or less sophisticated forms, they have established a rough and ready distinction between two forms of temporality. What is said to have disappeared with the collapse of the Soviet Union is not just an economic and political system. Nor is it simply a historical period marked by revolutionary hopes. What disappeared, so it is said, is a certain model of temporality: precisely the model of a time driven by a process of unveiling the truth and a promise of justice. What remains is nothing but the reality of a time now stripped of any immanent content, to be realized and restored to its ordinary course. The latter is open to various descriptions and evaluations. Our governments and the dominant media have greeted the advent, finally, of the age of expert management of the present and its immediate extension, calculating the prospects for prosperity afforded by measures taken over the next six months and destined to be verified in these months. Some disillusioned intellectuals have regarded this as the gloomy reality of a post-historical world characterized by the exclusive reign of the present, a present in which consumption and communication reign supreme. In any event, official optimism and prevailing catastrophism share the same vision: of a time that has bid farewell to the great hopes and bitter disappointments of the time of History inflected by a promise of justice. With some success, a historian suggested calling this new relationship to time 'presentism'.[1]

However, it soon emerged that this allegedly absolute present had not so easily rid itself of the passions generated by the burden of the past or the promises of the future. The countries liberated from the communist empire of the future soon found themselves afflicted by the revival of national grand narratives and ethnic or religious ancestral hatreds. The pacific Western states witnessed the return of histories that seemed to have been forgotten: histories of the threats posed by human beings of different races, colours and religions. But the putative reign of the pure present was also going to reveal itself as a war between

---

1   See François Hartog, *Régimes d'historicité: Présentisme et expériences du temps* (Paris: Editions du Seuil, 2003).

the burden of the past and the demands of the future that lie at the very heart of economic rationality. In fact, it was not long before we were told that expert, realistic management of the free market required sacrifices in the present to ensure future prosperity or avoid impending catastrophe: sacrifices that particularly concerned those whose working time was remunerated in wages, and who had grown used to retiring from work at a fixed age. The simplistic opposition between past illusions and the solid realities of the present was thus called into question by a division within the present. Obviously, we might regard this as the eternal mendacity of rulers, and conclude that the 'end of grand narratives' was nothing more than the narrative apt to ensure the permanence of exploitation. But explanations in terms of falsehood are always rather limited. It seems to me more useful to take this conflict of times seriously. What grounds the permanence of domination, but is also common to the time of 'grand narratives' and the time that claims to have abolished them, is a division within time itself. For time is not simply the line stretching between past and future – a line that can be infused with promises or reduced to its bare reality. It is also a hierarchical distribution of forms of life. And this is what emerges with the utmost clarity when people purport to revoke History's promises of unveiling and justice. It is not the lies of ideology that conceal reality. It is the way of narrating the progress of time that obscures the distribution of temporalities that grounds its possibility.

To understand this point, we must go back to the text I mentioned earlier – Aristotle's *Poetics* – which, for the Western world, established the principles of fictional rationality, and thereby constructed a model of intelligibility of human action whose range far exceeds the sphere of self-professed fictions. What is specific to the poet, says Aristotle, is the construction of a fiction – that is, a structure of causal connection linking events in a whole. Now, this construction presupposes a choice between two temporalities. For there are two ways of narrating. There is what Aristotle calls *historia*, which is often translated as 'chronicle' in order to avoid any confusion. *Historia* narrates how things happened empirically, as contingent events, one after the other. For its part, poetry is 'more philosophical': it does not say how things happened, but how they *might* happen, how they happen as a result of their own possibility.[2] Thus it constructs a specific time wherein the sequence of facts is identical to that of a chain of causes and effects. The time of fiction is organized in accordance with two types of series, which are also two types of reversal: a reversal of the situation, which changes from fortune into misfortune or, more rarely, from misfortune into fortune; and a reversal in knowledge, which passes from ignorance to knowledge. This is how time is linked to knowledge and justice. Tragic characters pass from fortune to misfortune not as a result of some divine

---

2   Aristotle, *Poetics*, 1451 a36–b10.

curse, but because their actions produce effects that are the reverse of those expected. And, in suffering these effects, they attain knowledge of what they did not know.

Clearly, the knot of these four notions – good fortune, misfortune, ignorance, knowledge – furnishes a matrix of rationality whose field of application can cover real changes in our societies as well as the plots invented by poets. Not for nothing does the causal rationality of fictional action have two equivalent modalities: it can be necessary or possible. The necessity of factual series and the verisimilitude of poetic creations pertain to the same form of rationality. But it is worth stressing the division of the temporalities that sustain this model of rationality. This division pits a rational time of fiction, where things are connected by causal links, to a time of ordinary reality, where they simply happen one after another. The hierarchy of times that grounds poetic privilege also defines the conditions of causal rationality. The latter has its place when we leave behind the universe of those who live from day to day. The hierarchy of times that grounds the rationality of human action corresponds to a hierarchy of places separating two categories of human being. There are those who live in the time of events that might happen, the time of action and its ends, which is also the time of knowledge and leisure. From antiquity to the nineteenth century, they have been referred to as active men or men of leisure. And then there are those who inhabit the time of things that happen one after another – the circumscribed, repetitive time of those dubbed passive or mechanical men, because they live in the universe of mere means without sharing in the ends of action any more than they do in leisure, which is an end in itself. The rationality of the horizontal unfolding of time is based on a vertical hierarchy that separates two forms of life, two ways of being in time – as we might simply put it, the way of those who have time and the way of those who do not.

The justice of time is thus twofold. There is the justice of the causal process conceptualized by Aristotle's *Poetics*: the justice that causes active men to pass from good fortune to misfortune and from ignorance to knowledge. And there is the other justice that silently supports it: the justice which is the subject of Plato's *Republic*. It consists in an orderly distribution of times and spaces, activities and capacities, and is based on a precondition stated by Plato at the very outset of the narrative about the foundation of the city. This precondition is that artisans, who must not have time to go elsewhere, time to do anything other than the work which cannot wait, should be kept exclusively in the space of the workshop.

If we wish to understand the structure of the celebrated grand narratives, and the way it survives in the present that is said to have abolished it, we must bring out the dual nature of time as a succession of moments and a hierarchy of occupations. The fact is that the grand narratives of modernity rest upon a dual distribution of time. On the one hand, they cancelled the contrast between fictional

reality and the purely empirical character of the successive facts of *historia*. That is how History – with a capital
H – became a form of rationality and a promise of justice.
The narratives of historical progress and the Marxist narrative of History applied the model of causality reserved
by Aristotle for fictional creation to the succession of
historical facts. They dismissed the hierarchy of temporalities by subordinating the time wherein things happen one
after another to the rational form of a series of causes and
effects. Marxism went even further: it located the rational
matrix of human activity in the obscure everyday world of
the production of material existence, and contrasted this
causal rationality from below with surface events pertaining to the glorious life of 'active men'. By the same token,
it connected the two reversals that formed the matrix of
fictional rationality differently. With a few exceptions, the
tragic bond equated the transition to knowledge with a
transition to misfortune. What tragic heroes learned at the
end of the story was the error that caused their misfortune.
By contrast, the new science of history heralded a transition from the misfortune of the experience of exploitation
to the happiness of liberation, secured thanks to the knowledge acquired of the law of necessity. A privileged link was
thereby asserted between necessity and possibility: the
necessary development of forms of exploitation yielded a
knowledge of necessity that made it possible to be rid of its
sway. History thus became the narrative of a positive conjunction between the unfolding of time, the production of

knowledge and the possibility of justice. Historical development itself produced a science of development that enabled historical agents to play an active role in transforming necessity into possibility.

Unfortunately, it was not long before the hierarchy of temporalities that the science of history purported to dismiss reappeared at its heart. For the very historical process that created the conditions for the future also constantly created new forms of divergence and retardation. Not only did it expel certain classes back into the past, thereby transforming them into obstacles to the advent of the future. It also operated at the very heart of the present to separate it from itself. The same laws that generated the system's functioning generated misrecognition of it. In everyday experience, and in the ways of seeing, thinking and acting of those who shared it, these laws reproduced the veil of ideology which kept people at a distance from knowledge of the real movement of historical forces. The same necessity that created possibility reproduced its impossibility. And the science of history had to internalize this double bind. It had to be simultaneously the science of the conditions of possibility of the future and the science of its recurrent impossibility. The hierarchy of temporalities that had previously separated two worlds now separated two ways of inhabiting the same world. A single historical process was lived in two ways. There were those – the minority – who lived in the time of science, the time of necessity known and transformed into an instrument of action. And then there were those – the majority – who lived in the time of ignorance, the time of succession and repetition that is the lot of passive human beings, oscillating between resignation to an ever identical present, nostalgia for a vanished past, and impatience for a future whose conditions were not yet ripe.

The heart of 'grand narratives' was thus not mere faith in a future that was to result from historical necessity. It was the inner splitting of that necessity, which was both a condition of possibility and a condition of impossibility. The science of historical necessity was knowledge of the possible destruction of capitalist domination and knowledge of its necessary reproduction and indefinite postponement of that destruction. This split was itself grounded in the duplication of time, in the present of divergence, in the present of the hierarchy of times, lodged at the heart of a time supposedly moving towards the end of domination.

It is clear, then, that neither the narrative of historical necessity nor the split that haunts it has disappeared in an absolute reign of the present. What the present offers us is a rearrangement of the interplay between necessity, possibility and impossibility. While the end of the Marxist grand narrative was loudly trumpeted, capitalist and state domination adopted its hard core – the principle of historical necessity – for their own purposes. Submission to this necessity, and comprehension of it, were more than ever made the sole route to any future happiness. This happiness, it is true, no longer took the forms of reversal and

rupture. On the contrary, it took the form of an optimi-
zation of the existing order. But we did not thereby find
ourselves in the kingdom of the sheer present. Historical
necessity received a new name. It was now called globalization. And globalization still seemed to involve a time
determined by its immanent end, which was no longer revolution, but the triumph of the global free market. Yet that
triumph could not be left exclusively to the 'freedom' of
this market. It demanded sacrifices. It did not simply mean
adapting to the ebb and flow of the market. More profoundly, it involved synchronizing two times: the rational
time of the global process of capitalist production and distribution of wealth and the empirical time of individuals
used to the temporality of things that happen 'one after
another' – for example, the moment of pay after hours of
work and the time of retirement after years of work. Obviously, it was the second that had to be synchronized with
the first. The set of measures directed to this end received
a name in the new grand narrative that was the counter-
part of 'revolution' in the old one. It was called 'reform'.
The meaning of this singular noun must be underscored.
It used to be commonplace to contrast the empirical
modesty of reforms with the abstractions of revolutionary
programmes. But 'reform' in the singular, as understood
today, is something quite different from a set of empirical
measures. It has become another master-signifier, another
symbol of historical necessity and its necessary conflict
with temporalities that are not in harmony with it. Here,

once again, the so-called liberal narrative has slipped into the temporal forms of the Marxist narrative. In the nineteenth century, Marx and Engels frowned on those artisans and petit-bourgeois who were attached to outdated social forms resistant to the development of capitalism, thereby delaying the socialist future of which it was the bearer. At the end of the twentieth century, the scenario was revised in such a way as to change not the form, but the characters. The condition of future prosperity was the liquidation of the legacies from an archaic past that went by the names of labour codes, employment legislation, social security, pension systems, and public or other services. Those blocking the road to the future were workers who clung to relics from the past. To punish this sin against the new justice of the time, it was first necessary to rename it. The social conquests of the past were re-baptized 'privileges', and war was waged on the privileged egotists who were defending their inherited benefits and short-term interests against the future of the community as a whole. Perfectly logically, a number of French intellectuals mobilized the arguments of Marxist science in the service of a right-wing government at war with the 'privileges' of the past. Their judgement was still rooted in a sense of historical necessity, and it was of little moment if this necessity now led to the triumph not of the socialist revolution but of the capitalist free market. Supposedly extinct, the grand narrative was thus reappropriated by guardians of the order it was intent on destroying.

It is true that a competing version of this narrative
existed, which reasserted itself as a critique of the time of
Capital. But this critique had itself been revised. Rather
than detecting in the development of capitalism symptoms
of its future collapse, it demonstrated capitalism's ability
in all circumstances to renew itself and turn any resistance
to its own advantage. And, at the heart of this reproduction, it also implicated inhabitants of the time of things that
happen one after another. It certainly did so conversely to
the official narrative, which condemned backward people
incapable of adapting to the time of the global market.
Instead, the critical narrative rebuked them for being too
well adapted to it and meeting its requirements either by
passively internalizing the values of consumerist freedom
and flexible personality, or by pitting against them lib-
ertarian values whose effect was to shatter the forms of
traditional authority that once limited the sway of the
free market. On the one hand, the critique of commodity fetishism, the consumer society and the society of the
spectacle, initially forged to dismantle the mechanics of
the system, now served to blame 'democratic individuals',
making their behaviour responsible for the permanence
of the system. On the other, rebellious anti-authoritarian
movements were accused of forging the modes of subjec-
tivation required by the new forms of capitalism. Such,
notably, was the argument of a highly influential book by
two sociologists, *The New Spirit of Capitalism*. According
to its authors, against the tradition of social critique rooted

in solidaristic working-class values, the revolting students of 1968 had affirmed an 'artistic critique' resting on the individualistic values of autonomy and creativity. Their revolt had thus given capitalism the means of regenerating itself following the crisis of 1973, by integrating those values of creativity and autonomy into the new forms of project-based participation and flexible management.

The critical narrative thus becomes the flip side of the official narrative. It tirelessly shows how the system reproduces itself ad infinitum, absorbing every form of subversion to make it a motor of its own development. This demonstration lends itself to two kinds of scenario: a scenario of repetition that favours constant validation of the demonstration of the necessary process; and a scenario of catastrophe that transforms the circle into a descending spiral and the demonstration of knowledge into a prophecy of disaster, displaying a humanity of flexible individuals and narcissistic consumers en route to a Last Judgement where it will expiate its sins against the order of the time. In the last analysis, the time of a causal process resulting in a reversal has been split into two times which, in their different ways, exclude any possibility of it: a time of eternal repetition and a time of decline and catastrophe.

One of these narratives reduces the tribunal of history to the science of the remedies that are to ensure the health of our societies. The other transforms it into the last judgement of humanity. But they concur on a certain way of naming necessity today. Both call it 'crisis', while offering

very different versions of it that nevertheless have something in common: their distance from what was understood
by the word in Marx's day. Then, crisis was the concrete
revelation of the contradiction informing a system, which
would then sweep it away. Now it is something quite different. It is the normal condition of a system governed by
the interests of financial capital. In a sense, it is simply the
name of the historical necessity called globalization, which
dictates the destruction of all obstacles to the triumph of the
free market. Yet this normality operates only by invariably
standing on the edge of the precipice, like that which only
lives thanks to the constant vigilance of scientists. Crisis
thus rediscovers its initial, medical meaning, but at the cost
of a radical divergence from what the word meant in the
Hippocratic tradition. In that tradition, crisis referred to
a very specific time: the final moment of an illness, when
the doctor had done everything within the remit of their
science and left the sick person on their own to fight the
battle from which they would emerge either dead or cured.
The medical temporality of crisis was used by literary
fiction to construct its own times and contretemps. Thus,
in *L'Éducation sentimentale* Madame Arnoux, seated at her
son's bedside, awaits the crisis while Frédéric paces round
their meeting point and insurrection rumbles in Paris. In
today's grand narrative, crisis is no longer the end of the
illness. It is the pathological state itself. And this pathological state is identified with the regular functioning of an
economic and social system. The crisis is not simply the

fact that the financial powers that live off debt sometimes experience difficulty obtaining repayment from those from whom they have withdrawn the means of paying. It is a whole system of domination identified with an order of rational time management at the price of declaring this rationality under constant threat from the incompetence and improvidence of those who live in the world of things that happen one after another. The economic crisis must thus be transformed into a social, and ultimately anthropological, crisis. Crisis comes to refer simply to the normal state of the world. However, the fact that it is called crisis makes it possible to assign it in its entirety to the attentive, uninterrupted care of doctors. In truth, these 'doctors' are themselves merely the holders of economic power and state power who manage the order of things. And the illness they treat is nothing other than the good health of a system of exploitation and domination. But the fact that it is called crisis widens the gap between two categories of human being: those who inhabit the pathological time of succession, where 'crisis' means wage reductions, the loss of employment and welfare benefits, and an inability to repay debts; and those who live in the time of science, where 'crisis' defines both the pathology of the sick person in need of treatment and the capacity of science not to cure but to manage it. Once again, as always, the grand narrative of the justice of time boils down to the gap between the form of life of scientists who master the time of ends and that of the ignorant imprisoned in the time of the everyday.

Just as the ignorance of the person who endures time is also the fault of debtors incapable of repaying their debt, the identity between the health of the system and the illness of social rejects is readily transposed into the catastrophist narrative of the crisis of civilization that provides the official narrative with a 'critical' lining.

People can proclaim the 'end of grand narratives' all they want. The narratives that rationalize domination, and those that purport to contest it, remain equally dependent on the fictional logic that dates back to Aristotle. No doubt, the scenario of a righting of wrongs is no longer on the agenda, replaced as it has been by the medical scenario of a normality on the verge of catastrophe. But we remain within the narrative of a necessary sequence grounded in a hierarchy of temporalities. In the shadow of so-called 'presentism', the powers of the state, finance, media and science endlessly create the gaps that reopen the distance between those who live in the time of the knowledge that delivers justice and those who live in the time of ignorance and error. Official discourse and critical discourse, the fiction of progress and that of decline, always revolve in the circle of necessity and ignorance of necessity. To escape this scenario, it is perhaps worth performing a sidestep and rethinking the 'justice of time' starting with its core: the hierarchy of temporalities, but also the struggle to abolish it. This is the shift I have sought to conceive in terms of forms of working-class emancipation and the theory of intellectual emancipation.

To work on forms of working-class emancipation is to encounter the fundamental reality of time as a form of life. That, in particular, is what I learned in the manuscripts I have often commented on by the carpenter Gauny: the most profound line of separation runs between those who have time and those who do not. The hierarchical distribution of times not only subjects the latter to the compulsion of exploited labour. It also gives them a body and a soul, a way of being in time and space, of moving their body, of directing their gaze, of speaking and thinking adapted to this compulsion. That is why emancipation is, in the first instance, a recapture of time, a different way of inhabiting it. This is what Gauny does when making a narrative of his working day. The working day is not merely the fragment of the capitalist process of exploitation that can be divided into the time of the reproduction of labour-power and the time of production of surplus-value. It is also the daily reproduction of the way of being of those who 'do not have' time. Now, this time is in principle excluded from the universe of narrative: nothing normally happens in it other than repetition of the same gestures. To recapture time is to transform this succession of hours where nothing is ever going to happen into a time characterized by a multitude of events. In Gauny's narrative, the working day is precisely a time in which something happens every hour: a different hand gesture, a gaze that strays, causing thought to wander, a thought that arises unexpectedly and changes the rhythm of the body, a play of affects prompting translation of the servitude or freedom experienced into a variety of gestures and contradictory sequences of thoughts.[3] Thus is generated a whole series of positive divergences from the normal time of reproduction of working-class being. And these divergences can be assembled into a divergent temporal sequence. In and through this dramaturgy of gestures, perceptions, thoughts and affects, it becomes possible for the carpenter to create a spiral which, in the midst of the compulsion of working hours, initiates a different way of inhabiting time, a different way of keeping a body and mind in motion. It began with the decision to put into narrative what was excluded from the universe of narrative, to change the way a worker is supposed to use their hands and words. And this decision to write presupposed an even more radical break: the carpenter had to take time he did not have, not simply putting off the moment of going to sleep each night, but crossing the line of symbolic separation that coincides with the least mutable of the empirical divisions of everyday time – the one separating night from day and rest from work. It was precisely this barrier that his brothers also had to push back in order to read and write, to meet and discuss ways of shattering the hierarchy of times.

The line of time may be divided from within. The fragmentation of things that happen 'one after another' contrasts with a different fragmentation that creates

---

3   See 'Le travail à la journée', in Gabriel Gauny, *Le Philosophe plébien*, texts collected and presented by Jacques Rancière (Paris: La Fabrique, 2017), pp. 53–8.

differences and breaks within the supposedly homogenous continuum. Each moment of this continuum is at once the point through which the reproduction of the hierarchy of times passes and the point of a gap, a break. For the official narrative, such ruptures are consistent with the process: the human beings of passive repetition are also the human beings of passing effervescence. But the moment is not the time of the ephemeral smugly contrasted with long-term sequences and the science of causes. It is also the power of generating a different temporality by redistributing the weights on the scales of the fates meted out to humans in accordance with the time they inhabit. It is here that the miniscule deviations which change the carpenter's working day are bound up with the barricades which challenge power. Individual emancipation – emancipation from a certain form of individuality – and collective emancipation – emancipation from a certain mode of collective being – feed off one another, and are based on the same power of the moment that creates a deviant temporal sequence. The narrative of the working day was written in the interval separating the Parisian revolution of July 1830 from that of February 1848. The power of the moment that generates a different time is the power of these revolutionary days, when the people composed of 'passive' human beings has forgotten the 'time which doesn't wait' and deserted the workshops to go into the streets and affirm their participation in a common history. In a famous text, Walter Benjamin referred to moments that explode continuous

time – the time of the victors – and took as their symbol
the Parisian insurgent firing on the clocks to stop time in
July 1830, just as Joshua stopped the sun. The anecdote
he glosses is obviously fabricated. But, over and above
dynamiting the dominant time, what those days yield is
the beginning of a different time, a different common time
born from the breaches made in the former: not a dream
time that would cause people to forget time endured or to
project a future paradise, but a time that is scanned differently, imparts a different weight to some instant, links it
to another moment by stepping over other instants, gives
itself different reference points in the past, constructs a
memory and, therewith, other futures even. The carpenter who reinvents his working day, and the insurgents who
interrupt the agendas of power and the routines of exploitation, counter the parcelling out that forever kept them at
a distance from their own time with a fragmentation that
gives them control of it and develops a new possibility.

The contrast between two ways of slicing up time is also
encapsulated, in the time of these microscopic or spectacular revolutions, in the extravagance of proposals for
intellectual emancipation. Joseph Jacotot taught that there
are two times of knowledge. There is normal time, the
time of pedagogy whose stages must be gone through in
the right order, starting with the original simplicity appropriate to a state of ignorance and arriving at the complexity
of knowledge. This path presupposes a guide who oversees
the whole process and consequently knows the order of

the stages and the pupil's capacity to follow it. The road leading from ignorance to knowledge is supposed by the same token to lead from inequality to equality. In reality, however, it interminably reproduces an inequality: the inequality between two ways of being in time. The time of emancipation is contrary to it in that it knows neither a zero point of original ignorance nor a fixed term to the progression. It thereby knows no definite order of stages constituting the knowledge reserved to the teacher. It is a new time that can start from any point, at any moment, and extend in unanticipated directions by inventing its own connections at every stage. This is what is encapsulated in the seemingly simplistic maxims that Jacotot pits against the logic of explanatory order: 'everything is in everything' and 'learn something and relate everything else to it in accordance with this principle: all human beings possess equal intelligence'. A new time can be created starting from something that can be found in everything. This something is not the particular thing that only possesses meaning with respect to the whole in which it is included, and whose path can only be shown to you by an experienced guide to time. It is already a totality in itself, a set of relations that can be unfolded, and whose unfolding paves the way for an unprecedented advancement.

Rethinking 'grand narratives' and their fate presupposes taking into account this form of temporality, which has been at the heart of practices and thoughts of emancipation. The fact is that the power of the moment which

creates a different temporal sequence has had a contradictory destiny in modern times. The progressivist tradition
consigned it to the bad side, that of the time of the ignorant
and impatient. In particular, the Marxist revolutionary tradition made it the time of spontaneous, ephemeral revolt
and future utopias, as opposed to the time of strategic action
based on knowledge of the historical process – even if, as
between February and October 1917, the strategists confis-
cated the dynamic of those 'passing moments' for their own
benefit. On the other hand, this shift on the axis of time
has been the principle of another revolution, the modern
revolution in fiction which is called literature. The latter
precisely called into question the Aristotelian opposition
between the time of causal connection and that of mere
succession. Virginia Woolf summed up this revolution best
in her essay 'Modern Fiction'. To the tyranny of plot and
its made-to-measure causalities she contrasts the truth of
those atoms of time that continually fall on our minds, and
whose arabesques it is the writer's duty to transcribe. Fiction's shift towards these showers of atoms and arabesques
has often been regarded as the peculiarity of an elitist literature complacently harping on the slightest sensations
of characters from elevated social circles. In the process,
what this rupture in the scale of times at bottom signified
has been forgotten: rejection of the opposition between
two sorts of human beings. The time of atoms falling
incessantly, contrasted with the time of things that 'might
happen', is not that of the moods of society people. It is

a time of coexistence that refuses the opposition between two types of succession – a time common to the humans said to be active and those deemed passive. It is a time that itself diverges, starting from any point whatsoever, in multiple, unpredictable directions. In Virginia Woolf it is the time the elegant Clarissa Dalloway shares in the streets of London with the anonymous lives that cross her path. It is the time of all those lives that struggle against the order that keeps them on the wrong side in the partition of forms of life. Behind the day of Clarissa Dalloway, who is taken up with preparing her evening reception, we should feel the presence of a different day: that of the peasant's daughter Emma Bovary watching through the window the constantly similar flow of hours and endeavouring to create for herself a story that shatters this repetition. And, behind her day, we should see that of the carpenter Gauny, intent on transforming hours of servitude into hours of liberty. Modern literary fiction has put at its centre this time where, at every instant, a battle is being waged between the misfortune that is servitude renewed and the fortune that is freedom gained: a time composed of a multiplicity of manifest micro-events whose coexistence and interpenetration are counterposed to the time of subordination specific to traditional fiction. But this also means that it has made the time regained by men and women doomed to the succession of days and hours its own time, the new material of its narratives, while abandoning its characters to the misfortune of creatures who vainly attempt to have the time they do not have.

The theory of the end of grand narratives conceals this unresolved tension between two ways of narrating time: as a totalization of moments in a sequence stretching towards an immanent end, or as a distribution and redistribution of forms of life. A theoretician of literature, Erich Auerbach, placed this tension at the heart of his history of Western realism. He set down two criteria for assessing the progress of that realism. One was the inclusion of individual destinies in an ever-changing totality of economic and social relations. The other was the accession of the most humble, the most nondescript, to the dignity of a subject of fiction. To his mind, the two criteria were supposed to harmonize: the ordinary individual was to rise to the dignity of fully fledged subject in line with their inclusion in the total dynamic of the economic and social world. Yet the history actually ended with the dissociation of the two, its point of arrival marked by an insignificant moment one evening of a holiday on the island in Virginia Woolf's *To the Lighthouse*. And it was in the stress on this ordinary moment that Auerbach saw the promise of a world of equality.

The narratives generated by our age on the relationship between global time and the time of individual lives scarcely seem in a hurry to confront such aporias. They describe a straightforward conformity between the time of individuals and that of the global system. They do so once again using the two opposed variants of the Marxist narrative. Some pursue the Marxist vision of ideology: they describe a perfect fit between a neoliberal subjectivity or flexible individuality, formed by the values of autonomy and creativity, and a global logic of capitalism, exploiting the illusion of individuals who believe they are freely managing their own time and activity to ensure its control over labour time – now coterminous with a whole lifetime. Others pursue the Marxist vision of capitalism fashioning the conditions of its own abolition, and draw the conformity in the opposite direction: they make these 'flexible individuals' 'cognitive' workers who are already possessors of the means of production of a capital that has become immaterial, and identifiable with the communism of the collective intellect. These contrasting versions of the correspondence between the time of individuals and the time of the system seem equally inattentive to the more complex forms of experience of time that characterize our present. The word 'precarity', generally used to encapsulate them, is at once exact and inadequate. Precarious time is not only a time full of holes, increasingly marked by speed-ups and slow-downs, by transitions from work to unemployment, and by all kinds of part-time and temporary work. It is also a time when individuals live the intertwining of several heterogeneous temporalities – for example, that of wage-labour and that of study, of artistic creation and odd jobs from one day to the next; a time in which those who have been trained for one kind of work and do another, work in one world and live in another, proliferate. We can describe this time as composed of intervals, taking the word in a double sense: intermittent work,

but also intervals between several temporalities. It is by
starting out from these intervals that it is possible to think
the new forms of interruption of the dominant time. An
interesting symptom of it was afforded in 2003 in France
by the movement of the so-called *intermittents du spectacle*
in the entertainment industry. In a sense, the controversy
over their compensation scheme only applied to a particular category of workers – artists whose time is divided
between the visible labour of participation in performances
and an invisible labour of preparation. However, some of
the actors in this movement stressed that their problem was
not specific to them: occasional work was becoming the
general form of casualized labour much more widely. And
at stake in the struggle was the construction of a new form
of common time in wider conditions of time with gaps and
heterogeneous temporalities.

It would be worth studying from this point of view the
forms of collective protest that marked the 2010s, from the
Arab Spring to the Occupy movements in Madrid, New
York, Istanbul, Athens, Paris and a number of other cities.
They have generally been analysed through the dominant
temporal grid which, on the horizontal axis of a unilin-
ear time, contrasts the transient character of spontaneous
movements of rebellion with long-term strategies based on
analysis of historical development. It seems more useful to
me to analyse them from the viewpoint of the division of
times. The very noun 'occupation' invites us to do so. The
word refers not simply to a relation to space, but to a way

of employing time. It thus involves the 'justice' of time that is assigned to a type of temporality. The justice of Plato's republic was precisely a distribution of occupations – of ways of employing one's time peculiar to each class. For artisans, it consisted in remaining in the workshop and engaging in the activity to which they were destined by birth, so as to satisfy the requirement of work that does not wait. It is this order of occupations, inscribed in the very materiality of places and the very flow of time, which workers in the modern age have challenged. Striking and occupying was not only a weapon in the struggle against economic exploitation, but also a subversion of the distribution of spaces, times and capacities that legitimized it. Recent occupation movements still work on the relationship between space and time. But occupation today is no longer the decision to spend time occupying the point of production. Instead, it is an attempt to overcome a dispersion of work spaces and times. Its theatre is no longer sites devoted to intensive production. The latter have been erased from the map of the visible. It occurs in intervallic spaces, in squares and parks normally given over to traffic or strolling. In these spaces of indeterminate temporality, those whom the new forms of capitalism have dispersed into a multitude of discordant places and times strive to recreate a common space and time. Occupied squares have thus afforded a potential meeting point for different experiences of fragmented time, bound up with a precarious condition variously common to the small vendor on a Tunisian street, whose suicide sparked the Jasmine Revolution, and the unemployed graduates in the squares of Madrid or New York. But these occupation movements have also offered an opportunity for an encounter between multiple forms of reappropriation of time, as if, after a fashion, the new modes of political action were employing the forms of coexistence of temporalities in city streets that the literary revolution opposed to the tyranny of plot. There are the interruptions of the normal flow of hours and activities symbolized by the performance of the 'standing man' in Taksim Square, facing the façade of the Atatürk Cultural Centre for eight hours without moving, thereby proposing a new form of unity between the time of artistic performance and that of political action. There is the time of the assembly, which symbolizes an alternative community, and time devoted to organizing an everyday life at once ordinary and situated in a space–time of secession. And there is the attempt to maintain over time moments of reconstruction of a common form of life in experiments in production, exchange, circulation of information, transmission of knowledge, and delivery of care that build networks of solidarity in the conflicts of the present, which is also the anticipation of a form of life still to come, a common form of life freed from the hierarchy of times and abilities.

It is not my intention here to judge the effectiveness of these forms of interruption of the dominant time or construction of different temporalities. It is enough that they invite us to rethink the way we narrate the time in which this effectiveness is measured. Contrary to analyses that proclaim the end of grand narratives and the exclusive reign of the present, I have sought to show how the fiction of historical necessity continues to structure the dominant time – the time of domination – at the cost of transforming promises of liberation into disillusioned registration of the order of things, or into prophecies of ultimate disaster. I have also sought to recall how this fiction of necessity is rooted in a hierarchical distribution of temporalities and life forms that it helped to renew. I have suggested a different way of thinking time, starting out from the singularity of moments when this hierarchy finds itself suspended, halted or diverted in the individual experience of a working day, in the novel in moments of inactivity, or in assemblies of crowds that interrupt the normal course of things.

2

MODERNITY REVISITED

The so-called modernist vision identified artistic modernity with an affirmation of the autonomy of art and the concentration of each art on its own specific medium. I have already had occasion to show how this 'modernity' is far removed from the actual changes undergone by the arts, the forms of existence of the arts, and thinking about them over the last two centuries. I shall, therefore, not repeat that here. Instead, I would like to focus on the fundamental ambiguity of this notion, which consists in the relationship it establishes between a practice called art and a time defined as modern. In order to affirm what it judges to be the modern revolution in art, the modernist doxa has to conceive this revolution within a history where the notion of art retains the same meaning from the time of cave paintings to the present. Now, this is precisely not the case. Art is itself a determinate historical configuration. It only exists as such within a specific regime of identification that makes it possible for performances or products, created by various techniques for different ends, to be perceived as belonging to one and the same regime of experience. This is not simply a matter of the 'reception' of works of art, but of the fabric of experience within which they are produced. This fabric is composed of institutions – performance or exhibition sites, forms of circulation and modes of reproduction – but also modes of perception and affect, concepts, narratives and judgements that identify them and give them their meaning. This regime of experience is what makes it possible for words, narratives, forms, colours, sounds, movements or rhythms to be perceived and conceived as 'art'.

Such a regime has not always existed. On the contrary, we can say that it has only existed in the Western world since the end of the eighteenth century. Certainly, many arts – that is, forms of knowledge and ways of applying them – existed prior to this. But they did not pertain to a common sphere of experience. Art as we name and understand it in our societies – Art in the singular, with a capital – was unknown to those who enjoyed themselves at the theatre, commissioned works from painters and sculptors, listened to religious concerts, or hired musicians for their feasts or ceremonies. This is not a merely lexical issue. Art did not exist as a common sphere of experience, not only because the practice of the arts was intended for different social purposes, but, above all, because these purposes were themselves part of a hierarchical division of human activities and of the human beings who engaged in them. The fine arts, which were distinguished from arts dedicated exclusively to utility, were the inheritors of the old hierarchy pitting liberal arts against mechanical arts. Now, this hierarchy was bound up not with the quality of the objects or performances produced, but with the quality of the persons who produced or practised them. The liberal arts were practised by so-called free men for their leisure. The mechanical arts were practised by artisans as a profession, for the utility of others and for their own subsistence. It is in relation to this hierarchy that the modern differentiation of art can be conceived and that we can understand the notions of representation and anti-representation. The modernist doxa is based on a simplistic idea equating representation with the servile imitation of reality, the better to contrast it with the modern emancipation of an art exclusively devoted to exploring its own medium. But representation was something quite different. It was a legislation regarding imitation, subjecting artistic practices to a set of rules that determined which subjects were suitable for artistic treatment and which form suited them, depending on their high or low character. This legislation involved the inscription of artistic practices in a system of concordance with the 'natural dispositions' of those to whom they were addressed. These 'natural' dispositions were peculiar to those whose nature was distinguished; they were the sign of a hierarchy of natures. Destruction

of the representative order is thus something quite different from the abandonment of figuration in the visual arts.
It is the destruction of a hierarchical order inscribed in
the very forms of the perceptible and the conceivable, the
destruction (in my terms) of a whole 'distribution of the
sensible'. This subversion of the very forms within which
artistic practices are perceived and conceived is what I have
called the aesthetic revolution. As a result of it, art exists
not simply as an essence common to all the arts, but as a
determinate historical configuration.

The historically determinate character of art is what is
forgotten by those who purport to historicize and politi-
cize an art they have initially posited as a general, timeless
concept. They think they can achieve this with the aid of
ideas of modernity, modernism and the avant-garde. Yet
these notions are utterly incapable of conceptualizing the
changes that have subverted the logic of the representative regime of art. On the contrary, it is on the basis of
those changes that it has been possible to elaborate them
as particular interpretations of the aesthetic revolution.
These interpretations possess two main features. First,
they translate the slow, impersonal changes of a regime of
experience into the decisions of conscious artistic volition.
Secondly, they connect these decisions with an attempt
to coincide with a temporal mutation. In its most general
formulation, modernism is defined as a desire to adapt to
the new rhythm of the time or to respond to a historical
exigency. But this desire has often been defined in very

simplistic terms. Thus, modernity has been identified with a will to embrace the simplified forms and accelerated pace of modern life, with a fascination with the efficiency of machines, the speed of cars, the brute forms of steel or cement, and the enchantments of electricity. In opposition to this, it is time we saw that the notions of modernity, modernism and avant-garde involve an interlacing of different temporalities, a complex interplay of relations between anticipation and belatedness, fragmentation and continuity, motion and immobility. This is because time is not simply the line stretching from a past to a future. It is also, and especially, a habitat. It is a form of distribution of the sensible, a distribution of human beings into two separate forms of life: the form of life of those who have time and the form of life of those who do not have it. This vertical dimension of time must be considered if we wish to understand what is at stake in modern political and aesthetic revolutions. And it is with regard to it that I would like to rethink what is at stake in descriptions of modernity and modernist programmes. I shall do so by focusing on a work that is emblematic of modernist volition, and hence emblematic of the actual temporal complexity of modernist time and its stakes. But, to that end, I must first of all set out the terms of the problem, utilizing two texts that illustrate contrary versions of modernism, antagonistic ways of displaying and dealing with its paradox.

I shall start with the text that furnished the dominant formulation of the modernist paradigm: the article by

Clement Greenberg, published in 1939, entitled 'Avant-garde and Kitsch'. The text has not wanted for admirers or critics. But both seem to have been inattentive to the paradoxical character of its argument. This paradox is readily summarized: Greenberg's analysis bases adherence to 'modernist' values on the impossibility of escaping a historical evolution that he describes as a process of decline. I recall how he formulates the terms of the problem. When a society's development renders it incapable of justifying its forms, it 'breaks up the accepted notions upon which artists and writers must depend in large part for communication with their audiences ... All the verities involved by religion, authority, tradition, style, are thrown into question, and the writer or artist is no longer able to estimate the response of his audience to the symbols and references with which he works.'[1] This is what had happened to the artists of antiquity, who succumbed to the subtleties of Alexandrianism when their art was no longer rooted in the collective life of city-states. This is what happens to modern artists in the era of advanced capitalism.

It is not difficult to recognize the matrix of this analysis: it adopts the terms of Hegel's analysis of the 'end of art'. When art is no longer the flowering of a collective form of life, it becomes (Hegel showed) a pure demonstration of virtuosity, sheer self-display. Art becomes its

---

1   Clement Greenberg, 'Avant-Garde and Kitsch', in Charles Harrison and Paul Wood, eds, *Art in Theory 1900–1990* (Oxford/Cambridge, MA: Blackwell, 1992), p. 530.

own imitation; and that signals the end of art. Now, it is precisely this 'end of art' that Greenberg makes the task of the avant-garde and the future of art. The avant-garde, he says, is increasingly detached from people's lives, increasingly doomed to imitating the very fact of imitating. The question then arises: how can a Marxist critique call a practice that is an effect of the necessary evolution of a society in decline 'avant-gardist'? Greenberg gives the question an answer that serves only to accentuate the paradox. There is, he says, an essential difference between ancient Alexandrianism and the modernist avant-garde: 'the avant-garde moves, while Alexandrianism stands still'.[2] This is a rather slender advantage if the only reason why the former moves is that it cannot but do so. In a sense, the avant-garde is obliged to be even more decadent than Alexandrianism. But, if so, says Greenberg, it is in order to counter the rise of another form of art that he calls rear-guard, even though it is perfectly attuned to the development of capitalist production and capitalist society. This is kitsch art and culture, which supplies cultural products manufactured for the sons and daughters of peasants now enjoying leisure time in the industrial metropolises for which no cultural tradition has prepared them. The paradox of avant-gardism and its struggle on opposite fronts are thus taken to extremes: avant-gardism is the movement that accelerates the impact of decadent capitalism on artistic creation to win the race

---

2   Ibid., p. 533.

against a 'rear-guard' which, for its part, is the expression of the forward march of capitalism.

This strange conception of modernity and avant-gardism is only intelligible if we regard it as an attempt to put a stop to the history of a quite different modernism and a very different vision of the avant-garde and its role. Greenberg certainly wanted to denounce a vision of fusion between the new art and the new life that to him was suspect. But he ignored the complexity of the montage of times underpinning this apparently simple fusion. To understand this complexity, we must probably go back to the diagnosis made a century earlier by another American thinker, likewise concerned, albeit in very different fashion, to respond to the Hegelian challenge of the 'end of art': Ralph Waldo Emerson. It is worth dwelling on the way that he construed the time of modernity in an essay entitled 'The Poet':

> Time and nature yield us many gifts, but not yet the timely man, the new religion, the reconciler, whom all things await … We have yet had no genius in America, with tyrannous eye, which knew the value of our incomparable materials, and saw, in the barbarism and materialism of the times, another carnival of the same gods whose picture he so much admires in Homer … Banks and tariffs, the newspaper and caucus, Methodism and Unitarianism, are flat and dull to dull people, but rest on the same foundations of wonder as the town

of Troy, and the temple of Delphos, and are as swiftly
passing away. Our logrolling, our stumps and their
politics, our fisheries, our Negroes, and Indians, our
boasts, and our repudiations, the wrath of rogues and
the pusillanimity of honest men, the northern trade, the
southern planting, the western clearing, Oregon, and
Texas, are yet unsung. Yet America is a poem in our
eyes; its ample geography dazzles the imagination, and
it will not wait long for metres.[3]

If I quote this manifesto at length, it is not simply because
its confidence in the poetry to come from within the very
heart of the prose of the new economic world is completely
opposed to Greenberg's disillusioned assessment and his
appeal to separate the task of the avant-garde from that
prose. It is because that confidence is far removed from
any naive faith in the simultaneous progress of machines
and men. On the contrary, it defines the task of the poet
within a radical intertwining of temporalities. Yet this
intertwinement is not merely the ingenious construction
of a theoretician. Much more broadly, it formulates the
complex interplay of the intertwined temporalities that
sustain the modernist project and the idea of the avant-
gardist subject charged with its realization.

---

3   Ralph Waldo Emerson, 'The Poet', in J. Slater, A. R. Ferguson
and J. Ferguson, eds, *Collected Works of Ralph Waldo Emerson, Vol. II:
Essays: First Series*, Introduction and notes by R. E. Spiller (Cambridge,
MA: Harvard University Press, 1971), p. 67.

At the heart of this complex temporality is a division of the present. On the one hand, Emerson affirms that inspiration for the new poetry is to be sought in the very chaos of the present. There is a reason for this: what is called chaos is the coexistence of heteroclite elements. The privilege of the present is the privilege of a time of coexistence. In the first instance, coexistence betokens heterogeneity. The poet's task is to encompass the multiplicity of the heterogeneous, concurrent phenomena that go to make up America's present. It is to weave the common thread that expresses the potential for common existence expressed by this diversity. More profoundly, however, the time of coexistence is a time without hierarchy. The democratized time of the aesthetic age is counterposed to the hierarchy of times governing the representative order that Aristotle summarized when contrasting fiction, which constructed a necessary or possible causal chain, with the mere chronicle of successive facts. The poet now has to give spiritual expression to a multiplicity of phenomena coexisting in a time without any hierarchy. But the present is not merely the unity that induces the coexistence of all these heterogeneous phenomena on an equal footing. This unity is itself divided. If the present is the coexistence of times, it is also their non-coincidence. The time has not yet produced the 'timely man', says Emerson. This expression does not simply mean that the moment has not yet come for the man who will express the new time; the issue is not one of belatedness and waiting. More radically, modern time is not contemporaneous with itself. The world of thought, spirituality and art inhabits it at a remove from a world given over to the prosaic explosion of economic appetites and interests. This non-contemporaneity of the modern is perhaps the most fundamental response to Hegel's diagnosis. Declaration of the 'end of art' rested upon a thesis of contemporaneity: for Hegel, modernity had been attained. The collective life of the people was now adequately expressed in the institutional forms of the economy, constitutional government and the civil service. And the spirit informing the development of history had found conscious expression in science. Collective life and the development of the spirit no longer needed to be represented outside of themselves, in the materiality of sculpted stone, painted surface or poetic metre. Art had thus lost its substantive content and found itself reduced to formal virtuosity. This is the thesis to which Greenberg's 'modernism' lends credence. But, to do so, it has to ignore the much more powerful and complex response that a century of art and thought had explored, of which Emerson's text furnishes one of the first, most radical formulations: modern time is a time that is not yet contemporaneous with itself. That is why it needs art, and that is what gives this art its character as an articulation of contradictory temporalities. According to Emerson, we are not at all in the time after, in the 'Alexandrian' time when art has lost its substantive content. On the contrary, we are in a time before. We are not yet modern.

But this 'not yet' is itself divided. It is at once the problem and the solution. On the one hand, it signifies that the prose of the American new world has not yet found its poetic or spiritual expression. We are confronted with the products of industry, the mechanisms of the economy and forms of life as prosaic things, situations and persons. We live in a world of things strictly confined to the egotistical economic relationship between immediate use-value and abstract exchange-value. These things, situations and forms must be given a different value, rendering them symbols of a new form of collective life. Such is the modern problem: constructing a new common sense, a new sensible fabric where prosaic activities receive the poetic value that makes them elements of a common world. It is not a question of waiting for time to give industrial and economic modernity its spiritual expression. It is a matter of anticipating, in the here and now, giving the shape of a world to a process that is as yet shapeless and chaotic. And this is where the problem affords a solution: the 'not yet' is not only a situation to be remedied, but also a reservoir of potentialities making it possible to construct a different common time for things and beings. Far from being in Alexandrian times, we are (says Emerson) living at the dawn of Homeric times. We are living at a time when the rationality of political economy and administration has not yet disciplined the chaos of material interests and prosaic activities. This chaotic material is what will enable the future poet to give ordinary things their symbolic value and hit upon the rhythms and images of the new poem. The spiritual thread that makes it possible to weave a new form of common sense is to be sought in the belatedness of modernity. From the noisy disharmony of the present we can extract the still-wild rhythm of a new life that will be the harmony of the future. Even if the term does not yet exist, this formulation of the poet's task furnishes us with the most precise idea of what an artistic 'avant-garde' might be, of what the historical project bearing that ambiguous name was. The vanguard is not the detachment that goes ahead of the main army. Still less is it the last battalion resisting the triumphant army of commodity culture. The avant-garde is located in the difference that separates modern times from themselves.

If Emerson's diagnosis is exemplary, it is because it is very close to the one offered at the same time by another thinker who is more readily associated with the idea of the avant-garde – namely, Karl Marx. The lecture given by Emerson in the winter of 1841–42 was published in its written form in 1844. And it was in the same year that the *Franco-German Yearbooks* published the *Contribution to the Critique of Hegel's Philosophy of Right*. Now, the core of Marx's argument consists in refuting the harmony between rational thought and a rationalized world formulated by Hegel in *Principles of the Philosophy of Right*. The present of German society and government is not, as Hegel would have it, proof of this harmony. On the contrary, it registers complete disharmony between two contemporaneous

times, one of which is in advance, while the other lags
behind. German philosophy has formulated a conception
of liberty that is in advance of its time. This thought has
no correlate in the contemporary reality of the Prussian
state, which is instead characterized by feudal and bureaucratic barbarism. But this discrepancy between the time of
conceived liberty and that of lived servitude is itself the
active principle of an unprecedented process of liberation.
By dint of its backwardness, Germany is in a position to
accomplish an unheard-of revolution, a human revolution
that skips the stage of merely political revolution. But it can
do so only on one condition: it must appropriate the revolutionary energy exemplified by the French without their
as yet being able to furnish a theoretical formulation of it
commensurate with the time. The alliance Marx proposes
between German thought and French action is, in fact,
an alliance between two forms of non-contemporaneity.
Employing the power of anticipation derived from the
backwardness of the present to construct an unprecedented
future – such is the temporal dramaturgy that Marx and
Emerson pit against Hegel's diagnosis of modernity at the
same time.

Art has no place in Marx's analysis. However, it is as
if Emerson's analysis were precisely anticipating the role
of anticipation assigned to their practice by Soviet artists
at the time of the revolution. We know that these artists
readily borrowed images of the modernity they sought to
ally with the new communist forms of life from America.

This betokened no mere fascination with the exploits of American industry or the seductiveness of a rationalized lifestyle. What fascinated them was the grand project of the new poem discovering its materials in the most ordinary phenomena of a new life still under construction and in the very dissonance of these phenomena. No doubt, Emerson was a forgotten thinker in the years following 1917. But his project was meanwhile popularized by a poet who was a key reference for all those at the time who wished to identify the modern world with the unanimous action of a crowd of equal men and women: Walt Whitman. It is here that the dream of correspondence between the new art and the new life finds its inspiration, even if this American-Soviet modernism came up against the Franco-German modernism whose legacy was claimed by the avant-garde party.

I should like to analyse this conflict of modernities on the basis of a film that quintessentially embodies the wish for an exact fusion between modernity and revolution, Dziga Vertov's *Man with a Movie Camera*. This film of 1929 attests to a conception of 'modernism' common to Soviet revolutionary artists despite their many differences. It proposed to use artistic means to produce not artworks intended for the pleasure of connoisseurs and bourgeois aesthetes, but new forms of collective life. *Man with a Movie Camera* is a revolutionary film. But a revolutionary film is not a film about revolution. It is a communist activity, one of the activities whose general articulation constitutes

communism, not as a form of political organization, but
as a new fabric of sensible experience. It is, therefore, a
film that does not tell stories, does not represent characters,
and even dispenses with words in order to be the pure connection between those activities that comprise the present
of life in a modern city, from waking in the morning, via
factory or shop work, public transport and street life, to
the evening's entertainment. Work about time is primarily
marked by selection of the day as its unit. It is certainly
not peculiar to Vertov. Alberto Cavalcanti with *Nothing but
the Hours*, and Walter Ruttmann with *Berlin: Symphony of
a Metropolis*, also employed it. But nor does this structure
characterize the documentary form in contrast to fiction.
James Joyce in *Ulysses* and Virginia Woolf in *Mrs Dalloway* made types of modern fiction with it. This is because
the day is not so much a stretch of time as a paradigm of
temporality. The story of a day illustrates the revolution
that Woolf proclaimed in her essay 'Modern Fiction'. In
it, she denounced the tyranny of causal emplotment, and
asserted, against the Aristotelian tradition, that the truth
of experience resided in the shower of atoms, the succession of sensible micro-events that happen one after another,
but above all alongside one another, in the absence of any
hierarchy. The time of the day in the big city is a time of
coexistence where the same kind of miniscule events happen
to all those who cross paths in the streets, while following different trajectories, or contribute from afar, without
seeing each other, to the same anonymous existence.

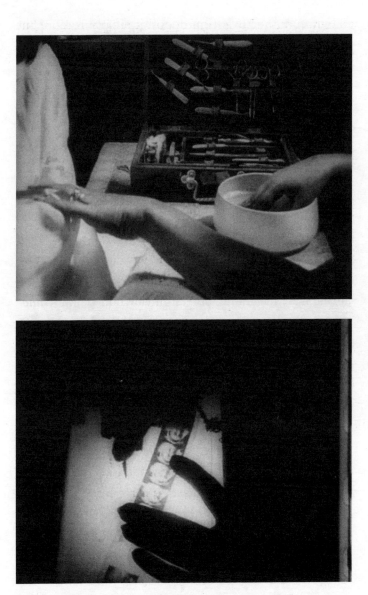

Dziga Vertov, *Man with a Movie Camera*, 1929.

However, Vertov's film does not simply recount the day's activities. It constructs a communist day, a day where these activities are driven by the same motor and compose a single whole, melting into one another. While the film begins at dawn and ends at night, its unfolding does not consist in a succession of activities over the course of the hours. On the contrary, it must radicalize the principle of coexistence by making all the activities equivalent and simultaneous. What counts is not any one of them in particular, but the capacity of each to assume the form of a sequence of gestures that is reflected in all the others and merges with them. That is why the film adopts a very specific narrative principle: throughout it, the camera is shown as one machine among others on which men and women are working. As for the cameraman and film editor, we see them making the same gestures as a female worker on an assembly line, typists in a typing pool, a cashier turning his cash register, a traffic officer operating his signals, or the employees in a telephone exchange connecting and disconnecting lines. All these activities are broken up into very short sequences, alternating at a fast pace, and merge into the same symphony of motion. That is why the film has sometimes been regarded as a naive futurist subscription to the modern idols of the machine, automation and speed; and this ultra-rapid montage has been equated with the Taylorist and Fordist breaking down of movements into precisely timed fragmentary gestures. The camera's attention to the actual gestures of an assembly-line worker in a cigarette factory manufacturing packets seems to illustrate Soviet artists' fascination with a Taylorist model that would make it possible to identify the principles of communist labour with those of artistic exactitude. In his text 'Biomechanics and the Actor of the Future',[4] Meyerhold had drawn all the conclusions of the new role assigned to art, which would no longer contribute to entertainment, but to the organization of collective work. To that end, artists themselves had to achieve optimal usage of their means of production, which in the case of actors was their own body.

Vertov's fragmentation of gestures initially seems to pertain to this Taylorist model. But, in reality, it functions completely differently. Taylorism breaks up a task into a finite number of complementary operations whose discrete exercise it seeks to optimize. Vertov's montage combines fragments of movements that are not complementary but simply equivalent. The heart of the day thus comprises a rapid montage of gestures whose only common property is that they are all the work of active hands: typists striking keys, the manufacture of cigarette packets on the assembly line, newspapers coming off the rotary presses, the work of miners attacking seams with their picks, that of the camera operator turning its handle, or the editor scraping and sticking the film – but also the work of a hairdresser and a manicurist in a beauty salon or the gestures of a shoe-shiner

---

4   See Edward Braun, ed. and transl., *Meyerhold on Theatre* (London: Bloomsbury Methuen Drama, 2016), Chapter 18.

in the street. The rapid montage of these fragments is not there to celebrate Taylorized labour or Soviet planning. Critics had already noted the fact in connection with Vertov's previous film, *The Eleventh Year*: the machines in it compose a grandiose symphony, but no one knows quite what they are producing, still less how this production might enter into some general plan. What the montage constructs is communism as the equivalence and fraternity of all the gestures of industrious hands. The montage of activities is, in reality, an extended parataxis that irresistibly recalls Walt Whitman's lists. In fact, it plays precisely the role that Emerson had attributed to the new poet, whose implementation was taken over by Whitman: weaving the spiritual thread that unites all activities, be they noble or vulgar, modern or archaic, bourgeois or proletarian. The flow of the homogenous present created by the accelerated montage in fact mingles heterogeneous temporalities. It is very difficult to consider nail-polishing in a beauty salon or the activity of a shoe-shiner as illustrations of the new Soviet life. But nail-polishing becomes communist when the film combines it with the editor's scraping of the film, which can also be combined with the miner's pick striking the seams. Vertov, who was unaware of Emerson but not of Whitman, applies the Emersonian principle: it is in the disharmony, the barbarism even, of intertwined temporalities that we are to find the thread capable of uniting the new community. He had applied it even more radically two years earlier, in *A Sixth Part of the World*. Causing a great scandal among the Soviet authorities, he had represented the reality of communist life in the Asiatic republics of the Soviet Union by assembling images of caravans of camels in the steppes and reindeer in the tundra, Kalmyk fishermen hauling in their nets, Siberian hunters drawing their bows, nomads eating raw meat dipped in blood that was still warm, and Muslims bowing down to pray. What is communist is not the nature of these activities, but the bond that unites them, starting from their very disparity.

Thus, a complex temporal interplay is set in train by this film. It is avant-garde in as much as, with the constitution of a common time, it anticipates the communist sensible world that, for Soviet leaders, could only result from a protracted process of construction. This common time is itself

Dziga Vertov, *Man with a Movie Camera*, 1929.

composed out of a multitude of movements that belong to heterogeneous temporalities, montages of the most traditional gestures with those of assembly-line work. All these movements can be made equivalent units in one and the same overall movement. It is specifically the art of movement that plays the role of the new poet by capturing all the activities and temporalities in the same rhythm. Cinema is, as it were, the movement of all these movements, the one that assembles them all, but also the one that fixes their commonality in symbols.

This operation of symbolization culminates in the film's final episode. Having constructed the common time of all the activities by means of montage, the film engages in a new operation: the montage is presented in a film theatre to those who have taken part in these activities during the day. Obviously, the film is not going to restart. What it presents to the spectators is a montage of symbols that condense the great symphony of the day. Some of these symbols are borrowed from the day's activities, but this is not true of the three ballerinas who emerge not as a spectacle, but as a symbol of the overall movement. Their dance only occupies a brief moment in the film. But this brief moment possesses sufficient symbolic weight to feature on the two posters designed by the Stenberg brothers to advertise the film in a very specific montage. The first poster combines a dancer's legs in motion with a camera tripod, while her eye is coupled with the mechanical eye of the lens. The second shows us a dancer caught up in an ecstatic movement, except that her body is composed of disjointed pieces: four detached body parts deployed as the wings of a helix the better to be projected into space, while a radiant head in the centre of the image expresses the utter euphoria of the movement. The symbol is therefore powerful. But it remains to be known exactly what it is a symbol of. It is not simply that of the collective energy of Soviet workers. Significantly, the dancer in the second poster is wearing high heels, which are more evocative of an emancipated American woman than a female Soviet shock worker. And the marriage that the posters, like the film, effect between the euphoria of dance and the motion of machines has nothing to do with the 'dance of machines' so popular at the time in the USSR, any more than it does with the futuristic cult of speed à la Marinetti. What is expressed in the dancers'

Vladimir and Georgii Stenberg, poster for
Man with a Movie Camera, 1929.

ecstatic movement is not the power of the collective or of industrial modernity, but simply the euphoria of movement for its own sake.

Such euphoria was embodied by a dancer who had died shortly before, and who had once sought to place it in the service of the Soviet Revolution: Isadora Duncan. Her dance was presented as an expression of free movement. Free movement is not movement freely decided by artistic volition. On the contrary, it is movement that is not a matter of choice, movement embracing that of a life which has never begun and knows no interruptions or stoppages. This continuous movement, which incessantly generates another movement, abolishes the very contrast between movement and rest. The equality of movement and rest has a long history in the aesthetic regime of art. It already characterized the aesthetic condition as defined by Schiller as a state of equilibrium between activity and passivity. But the conceptualization of this state of equilibrium was itself the product of a matrix image: Winckelmann's description of the Belvedere Torso, the torso of a now inactive Hercules, in which calm reflection on past exploits is expressed by the undulation of muscles, which merge into one another in the manner of waves endlessly rising and falling.[5] The wave, the perpetual motion that equals movement and rest – such is the model for Isadora Duncan's dance. Such is

---

5   Readers are referred to my *Aisthesis: Scenes from the Aesthetic Regime of Art*, transl. Zakir Paul (London/New York: Verso, 2013), Chapter 1.

Vladimir and Georgii Stenberg, poster for
Man with a Movie Camera, 1929.

also the model that inspires not only the performance of
Dziga Vertov's three ballerinas, but also the symphony of
the communist day in the factories and streets.

To think what, at first sight, is the disconcerting relationship between the immemorial motion of the wave and
the activity of the new communist life, we must go even
further back into the past, to the archaeology of aesthetic
paradigms that are also political paradigms. This equality
revokes the ancestral hierarchy of forms of life: the one
separating active men from passive men, separating them
in their way of being in motion as well as in their ways of
being at rest. In Book 8 of the *Politics*, Aristotle contrasts
two ways of being inactive: rest, or the break, the time of
relaxation required between two periods of physical exer-
tion; and leisure, or the free time of those not subject to the

compulsion of labour and rest. This hierarchy of inactivity was itself the flip side of a hierarchy of ways of acting. Leisure was the form of inactivity appropriate to so-called free or active men, who were capable either of projecting the ends of their activity far ahead, or of acting solely for the pleasure of asserting their capacity for action. For its part, rest corresponded to the way of being of so-called passive or mechanical men, because their activities were never anything but means of satisfying immediate needs. What the free movement of the wave emblematizes is the abolition of this hierarchy of times and movements, which divided humanity into two classes. What is modern is not the men or women embracing the rapid rhythm of machines on the horizontal axis of time, but the abolition of the hierarchy separating mechanical human beings from free human beings on its vertical axis. It is the non-hierarchical redistribution of the basic forms of sensible experience. The task of the avant-garde, as performed by Vertov, is to construct the new egalitarian sensorium wherein all activities are equal and form part of the same movement. This equality has but one condition: the movement ensuring it is a free movement, a movement that abolishes the difference between the 'free' and the 'mechanical', but also the separation between the ends and means of activity. Free movement presents itself as the appropriate form for identifying the 'modern' task of constructing the thread that links heterogeneous activities to the communist task of building a sensible world governed by equality, but at the price of calling into question what seems to be the motor of any construction – namely, voluntary action. Such is the paradoxical conclusion that the great thinker of modern choreography Rudolf Laban would draw from Isadora Duncan's discoveries, when, twenty years later, he concerned himself with applying the teachings of the art of movement to British industry:

> Movement considered hitherto – at least in our civilization – as the servant of man employed to achieve an extraneous practical purpose was brought to light as an independent power creating states of mind frequently stronger than man's will. This was quite a disconcerting discovery at a time when extraneous achievements through will-power seemed to be the paramount objective of human striving.[6]

This 'discovery', 'disconcerting' for anyone who seeks to reduce the movements of dance and those of industry to a single principle, makes identifying free movement, industry and communism even more problematic. The conflict of modernities then becomes a conflict of communisms. On the one hand, the non-differentiation between means and ends, specific to free movement, seems to define communism as Marx conceived it in the *1844 Manuscripts*: communism is a form of society where the generic activity

---

6   Rudolf Laban, *Modern Educational Dance* (London: MacDonald & Evans, 1948), p. 6.

of human beings – labour – has become an end in itself, rather than a mere means of survival. This is the sort of communism realized in the common movement that unites them by the gestures of cigarette factory workers, typists, telephone exchange employees, the manicurist or film editor, which is symbolized by the movements of the three dancers. But communism in motion has a condition: that each of these actions is disconnected from its particular temporality and from the particular ends it pursues. The communist industrial symphony pursues no end; it produces nothing but itself. In this, obviously, it is quite contrary to the strategic vision of the communist apparatus. For the latter, the communist identity of ends and means is a goal to be attained; and it is, first of all, necessary to establish its material conditions. Factory machines, workers' gestures and artistic performances are not equivalent expressions of free movement. They are tools which, in their various ways, serve to create the conditions for the communism of the future.

This opposition has readily been regarded as a manifestation of the eternal conflict between freedom of artistic creation and political authority. It is more accurate to see it as the conflict between two communisms, between two ways of constructing the very temporality of communism. From the standpoint of the party-state, communism cannot be anticipated. It can only exist as a result whose conditions must first be established. Pitted against this is an aesthetic communism for which, on the contrary, communism can exist only if it has first been anticipated in the construction of a common sensorium of equality. We know how this conflict ended up being resolved. The builders of 'real' – that is, state – communism urged artists to abandon the pretension to forge the sensible forms of the new community. For them, there could be but a single time – that of the before and the after, of means and ends, of work and rest. The task of Soviet artists was to assist the party's strategy by representing the workers' exertions, and entertaining them after their exertions. In short, they had to follow the logic of the representative regime of the arts and the hierarchy of temporalities on which it rested.

State repression of the modernist project paved the way for its ideological and artistic repression, which has, ironically, assumed the name of modernism. What is striking in Clement Greenberg's analysis is the way that he erases the dramaturgy of temporalities at the heart of the historical modernist project, to leave only a single temporality: the unidirectional development of capitalism, which yields both the solitude of an art bereft of any foundation of common values and symbols and the rapid development of kitsch culture. Thereafter this new-style modernism can ignore what renders it possible – the repression of an earlier modernism – and make Stalinist socialist realism the simple Soviet version of kitsch culture. Above all, it can restore the hierarchy of temporalities and forms of life contested by modernist artists, but also by emancipated workers and women from the popular classes desirous of a different life.

In this respect, Greenberg's genealogy of kitsch culture is enlightening. He regards it as a consequence of the exodus of the sons and daughters of peasants into big industrial cities. It is there that, along with strict factory schedules, men and women discovered the existence of a quite separate time, an empty time exceeding the rest necessary to restore their strength and identified with the leisure that had hitherto been the privileged time of 'active' men. In it, they discovered a new capacity, the capacity for experiencing the emotion peculiar to empty time: boredom. And this discovery led them to 'set up a pressure on society to provide them with a kind of culture fit for their own consumption'.[7] What answered this demand was the development of kitsch culture, which now threatens the 'great art' whose preservation has fallen to the avant-garde, at the cost of a headlong flight into decadence.

Thus is clarified what is ultimately at stake in the bizarre temporal construction underpinning Greenberg's 'modernism'. The disaster for art arrives, he tells us, when the sons and daughters of peasants or artisans find themselves in possession of leisure time without having the means to appreciate 'the values of genuine culture'.[8] This judgement comes down to restoring the old Platonic commandment: artisans must remain in their workshop and devote themselves to the only work for which the divinity has given

---

7   Greenberg, 'Avant-Garde and Kitsch', p. 534.
8   Ibid.

them the requisite aptitudes, because 'work does not wait'. Ironically, such might be the philosophical principle underpinning this retrospective modernism and inverted avant-garde.

3

THE MOMENT OF DANCE

To speak of a *moment* of dance presupposes making two distinctions. First of all, I do not intend to advance an aesthetic of dance in the usual sense of the word: a discourse defining the characteristics of some particular art on the basis of those of art in general. I would like to identify a specific time when dance was more than an art: it was a paradigm of art and of the relationship between art and life. This assumes a second distinction, concerning ways of conceiving the time of this relationship. In effect, philosophy has readily presented it as a time of the origin. It has proposed an ontology of the dancing body, identified with a narrative of the birth of art. This is the case with two philosophers of my generation. In his book *Alliterations*, Jean-Luc Nancy has analysed dance as the expression of an original separation. For his part, in *Handbook of Inaesthetics*, Alain Badiou has made dance a metaphor for thinking, the original expression of the body's capacity to display the event of thought before this event has even been given a name. In his phenomenological fashion, the former invites us to grasp the original movement of dance and the original movement of thought. In axiomatic fashion, the second (following Mallarmé) sets out the 'axioms' of dance. In both cases, the philosopher positions himself, in reality or in imagination, before a dancing body and undertakes to tell us what happens when this body is set in motion. For me, the beginning of dance and of reflection on dance is a dramaturgy of the retrospective. For such a dramatization of the origin of dance and of dance as origin to be possible, it must already be the case that the dancing body has been positioned within a certain form of visibility and a certain horizon of thought. These philosophical statements presuppose that dance has become a particular paradigm of art.

A paradigm of art is essentially two things. First, it is a paradigm of the relationship between what pertains to art and what does not pertain to it: for example, between a painting in a museum and a commodity in a shop; or, again, between bodily movements made on a stage and the gestures of a body in a workshop or on the street. Secondly, it is a paradigm of the relationship between thought and that which is not thought: the light of a picture, the development of a melody, or the movement of a body in a space. For a theoretician to position himself before a work of art and propose a theory of that art, there must already exist a whole implicit system of relations between thought, space, sight, light, sound and movement. Such a system is what I call a distribution of the sensible. What we call arts are particular knots within this distribution. They are determinate historical configurations. Art as the configuration of a determinate sphere of experience has only existed in the Western world since the eighteenth century. As for dance, we can situate the historical moment when it became part of art thus construed. It is not only the moment when it was added to the list of the arts included in that sphere. It is also the moment when it embodied a new paradigm of art: a new paradigm of the relationship between thought and its outside and between art and non-art. We can identify a 'moment' of dance historically and define it theoretically. The term does not simply refer to a period – between the 1890s and the 1920s – when dance came to be recognized as a fully fledged art. A 'moment' is not merely a division of time; according to the etymology of the word, it is also the movement generated by a certain balance or imbalance of weights on scales. To put it in my terms, it is a certain redistribution of the sensible: a new way of perceiving the performances enacted by certain bodies and of relating them to other performances and other modes of perception within a common world. This moment of redistribution, and the role played in it by dance, is what I should like to talk about.

For the sake of convenience, I shall start with a section of the film I have taken as a reference point in constructing my own understanding of what modernity might mean:

Dziga Vertov's *Man with a Movie Camera*. This is not obviously a film about dance or art more generally. It is a film that seeks to construct the common sensorium of a new life. But, for that very reason, it is interesting to start with the brief episode representing three dancers. Starting from there, we can in fact understand the role dance has been able to play not simply as art, but also as a form of movement symbolizing the overall movement of a new world.

The dance occurs at a very specific point, in the final sequence when the film returns to the movie theatre where it began. In the interim, it has followed the various activities that make up the ordinary texture of daily life in big cities, from waking in the morning to the evening's entertainments: those of factory workers, shop workers, bus conductors, traffic police, firefighters and many more. It has constructed the general movement that results from their interconnection. We have now reached the point where the synthesis of all the activities is presented in the movie theatre to those who have acted in them. The symphony of the communist day is condensed into a limited number of performances that are not so much moments of this day as symbols of the fusion of all these activities in a single comprehensive movement. Many of these symbols, it is true, are derived from actions that have punctuated the film, such as the gestures of the telephone exchange employees who both do their own particular work and symbolize the establishment of universal communication. But this is not true of the three dancers who suddenly appear on the screen. Their performance is not a reminder of an activity performed during the day or even the evening's entertainment. It does not belong to the chronicle of the day. It pertains to the film as such. Moreover, the image of it only appears superimposed on other images. It is there to synthesize and symbolize the collective symphony composed by all the movements and the common energy expressed in the gestures of hands and the movements of machines: in the whirling of the spinning machine and the smile of the worker, the gestures of the telephone employees, the movements of the trains and buses, the speed of the cameraman's motor bike or that of his hand turning the camera handle. This fusion of the energy of bodies and that of machines in a single apotheosis of movement is already symbolized in the posters for the film designed by the Stenberg brothers: in them a dancer's ecstatic movement is depicted as identical to that of machines, identical to the movement of a life that no longer knows any distinction between them. In symbolizing the commonality of all movements, the dance also symbolizes an idea of artistic modernity in accord with an idea of the communist new life.

The issue is in what, precisely, this consists. We might, in fact, regard this commonality of movements symbolizing the movement of a community as the modern version of a politics of movement whose paradigm was formulated by Plato in the *Laws*. This paradigm was the choral community wherein citizens materially express their unity by

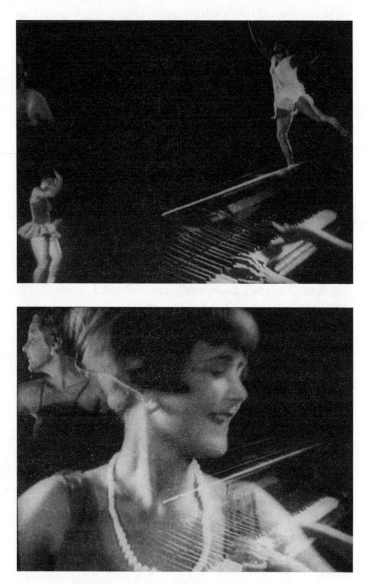

Dziga Vertov, *Man with a Movie Camera*, 1929.

participating in the dancing choir. This Spartan model of the active community was counterposed by Plato to the Athenian democratic model of the theatre, where citizens passively watch the play – that is, the falsehood of representation where actors express emotions they do not themselves feel, and which no one actually experiences since they are attributed by a poet to fictional characters. To this simulacrum of art, dance opposes the art of the active community, the direct expression of a form of life that does not know the separation, passivity and falsehood of the spectacle. This model of the choral community, which directly experiences and expresses the bonds of fraternity, was revived in the eighteenth century. It is what Rousseau, in his *Letter to d'Alembert*, pitted against the simulacra of the theatre, against its illusory happiness for which a people, turned into an audience of passive spectators, sacrifices the possibility of real happiness; and against its pseudo-lessons in morality that teach nothing but egotism and falsehood. But this rehabilitation of the Platonic *choreia* echoes a revolution proclaimed in the same year specifically in connection with dance. It was in 1758 that Jean-Georges Noverre published his *Lettres sur la danse et le ballet*. In them he denounces the art of ballet which, at the time of Louis XIV, had been codified as an interplay of noble attitudes, virtuoso movements and complicated figures symbolizing a whole aristocratic way of life. For Noverre, this putative aristocratic distinction was quite the opposite: it was a purely physical performance obeying a set of mechanical conventions that told no story and expressed no emotion. To become an art, dance must abandon exercises in elegant virtuosity and rediscover the ancient Roman tradition of pantomime. It must develop a language of gestures and attitudes capable of telling stories and expressing situations and feelings. It must represent characters and situations similar to those encountered in real life and in all social conditions. This reform of dance echoes the reform of dramatic art proposed by Diderot in *Conversations on the Natural Son*. In this way, the mechanical art of ballet and the conventional art of dramatic action would be dismissed together, in favour of a single art of the expressive body speaking the universal language of movement.

We know the role played by this idea of an expressive language of movement throughout the history of modern dance and performance, and of their endeavours to identify a new form of art with the invention of a new life. Not for nothing did one of the great teachers of modern dance, Rudolf Laban, pay homage to Noverre's 'ballet of action'. Not for nothing, either, was the idea of expression so strongly linked in 1920s Germany with the project of the new dance embodied, in particular, in Mary Wigman's *Ausdruckstanz*. It would therefore seem natural to include in this tradition the performance of the three dancers in a film that claims to be written exclusively in the language of movement and to condense the energy of all the movements that make up the new life of communism. However, this idea of dance is not one that can make it the movement expressing the new life. The reason is simple: following Plato, Noverre and Diderot contrast the truth of expressive movement with the falsehood of dramatic mimesis. But this movement was itself conceived as a language, a direct language of the body giving the emotions of the soul a vocabulary adequate to them. What they oppose to mimesis is thus a more exact language, a more radical mimesis. By contrast, the movement of Vertov's dancers is alien to any mimesis. It tells no story. It expresses no invisible truth of human emotions. Nor does it express unconscious forces moving bodies. It expresses nothing but movement: movement for movement's sake, free from any goal to be attained and from any particular sentiment to be expressed or any unconscious force expressing itself through it. It is not one of those 'machine dances' in favour in the USSR at the time, which were immortalized in a photograph by Margaret Bourke-White. Nor is it an expressive dance giving expression to the collective energy of the builders of communism by massed bodies in swarms that we find in some of Mary Wigman's choreography. It is simply a free movement that is its own raison d'être. And, for two or three decades, this is what the art of dance found itself illustrating and symbolizing at the same time: the art of free movement, the art whose performance is identical to the free deployment of movement.

The main question, obviously, is what this freedom means exactly, and how it manifests itself. We can understand this with the help of two emblematic figures who embodied the art of free movement, and who set the stage against whose background we can identify the performance of the dancing body with the activity of a new life. The first, whom I have already mentioned, is Isadora Duncan. She especially illustrated the idea of free movement. The latter is not the movement wherein artists express themselves by freely combining the gestures of their performance. A movement is not free merely by virtue of the fact that it is not determined by some external force. It is free when no force determines it, not even the force of a voluntary decision. It is free when it is its own generator. Free movement is a continuous movement that incessantly generates another movement. This continual movement repudiates Nietzsche's opposition between Apollonian appearances and Dionysiac forces underneath. Like Isadora Duncan, Vertov's dancers combine the two characteristics: they are varieties of Apollonian maenad, like her aroused by the frenzy already present in the calm, regular movement of the wave that breaks on the shore. The metaphor of the wave plays a key role in Isadora Duncan because in it the peaceful undulation of the line is equal to the frenzy of universal life. 'Freedom' of movement is the calm identity of opposites at the heart of the aesthetic regime of art. It received theoretical formulation in Schiller's definition of the aesthetic state as a balance between activity and inactivity. But the formula had itself been made possible by the analysis of free movement in

Winckelmann's paradoxical description of the Belvedere Torso. Winckelmann described an inactive Hercules. Deprived of the body parts required for action, the hero calmly meditated on his past exploits. But, because he no longer had a head, his thought was expressed exclusively by the undulation of his muscles, which merged into one another in the way that waves endlessly rise and fall in the sea. The direct relationship established by Winckelmann between the infinite character of thought and the incessant motion of waves precisely defines a paradigm of art in the aesthetic regime. And it is this paradigm that dance comes to illustrate. It is not simply an expression of the impersonal power of universal life. It also expresses a paradigmatic mode of the presence of thought in that which is alien to it.

The relationship between thought and non-thought must also be a relationship between art and non-art – to be precise, a relationship of equivalence between the performance of art and the movement of the new life, the revolutionary life. What renders the free movement of dance equal to the mode of existence of an emancipated community is the rupture it symbolizes in a hierarchy rooted at the deepest level of sensible experience: the one that distinguishes between two sorts of human being, so-called active human beings and those deemed passive or mechanical. The former could project ahead the goals of their action. Conversely, they could act solely for the pleasure of acting. They could thus savour leisure, the form of inactivity that is an end in itself. The latter know no form of activity but that which provides for life's immediate needs and no form of inactivity but the rest required between two expenditures of energy. The free movement of the dancing body thus emerges as the form of sensible exercise that cancels this hierarchy of bodies, movements and temporalities. The wave is its emblem and, perfectly naturally, its immemorial motion comes to express the new universe of industry that is the universe of electricity, that immaterial energy which animates the material world. The marriage of the dancing body and the machine thus makes sense. It is not a question of glorifying the machine, but of abolishing the hierarchy that separates mechanical human beings from free human beings. The 'mechanical' man is not the one occupied with machines, but (according to the etymology of the word) the man confined to the universe of means. The union of the dancing body and the machine symbolizes, on the contrary, a sensible universe where means and ends are no longer divorced. This non-differentiation is at the heart of the aesthetic regime of art. It finds exemplary formulation in the third definition proposed by the analytic of the beautiful in Kant's *Critique of Judgement*: '*Beauty* is the form of *purposiveness* in an object, so far as this is perceived in it *apart from the representation of an end*.'[1] But it is also at the heart of Marx's definition of communism, at the heart of the 'human revolution' that

---

1   Immanuel Kant, *Critique of Judgement* (Oxford: Oxford University Press, 2007), p. 66.

goes beyond a mere political revolution. Communism is the righting of the topsy-turvy world where labour, the generic activity that expresses the human essence, is transformed into a sheer means for the reproduction of human existence. It is the non-separation of means and ends. The fundamental identity of the aesthetic mode of experience and the communist mode of being receives adequate expression when the movements of dance – the quintessential aesthetic art – come to synthesize and symbolize the movements of the communist day, those equal movements that construct a new common world.

But the issue is not only knowing what the art of dance symbolizes, but also how it symbolizes it. The performance of the three dancers in Vertov's film is not the vital energy of the new community exploding onto the screen. It is an image of movement articulated in a montage with other images. Three features are significant in this respect. First, the dancers dance in superimposition. Their image appears above a piano. Lower down, we see the hands of a pianist on the keyboard and, behind these hands, another image and a double exposure: that of a woman conductor. When this last image fades, the keyboard is multiplied by its own reflection. The dancers are thus never alone. Another image always accompanies them and offers an analogy for their performance. Secondly, the images of the dance alternate with those of the audience – an audience comprising the day's workers, male and female. Thirdly, they are relayed by other symbols of continual movement:

the female telephone operators who endlessly connect and disconnect lines; the employees in a typing pool; traffic in the roads, planes in a carousel in the sky, or the wheel of the spinning machine on which a worker's radiant face is superimposed. The image of common movement is at once created, intensified and shattered by a constant interplay of relations between images. Thus, the dance does not afford a simple paradigm of unity. Instead, it offers a paradigm of relationality. It is invariably linked materially, or referred symbolically, to something other than itself.

To understand this relationality, it is worth dwelling on the performance of another dancer, and the commentary on it by a poet who seemingly has nothing to do with the communist revolution. In 1893, on the stage of the Folies Bergère, Mallarmé watched a show by another American dancer – Loie Fuller – and set about formulating the principles of a 'restored aesthetics' that might be derived from the whirling movements she made with the veils of her dress, bathed in colour by the coloured light projections. These principles were those of an exemplary identity of opposites, of a perfect intertwinement of times. For Mallarmé, her dance was a fusion of the 'intoxication of art' and 'industrial accomplishment'.[2] It hailed from the United States, but was Greek in origin, classical in so far as it was absolutely modern. It was modern, that is, freed

---

2   Stéphane Mallarmé, 'Autre étude de danse: Les fonds dans le ballet', *Divagations*, in *Oeuvres complètes*, vol. 2, ed. Bertrand Marchal (Paris: Gallimard, 2003), p. 174.

from the representative form of ballet, because it took place on a stage bereft of any scenery, did not tell a story, and did not imitate the feelings of any character. It was simply the unfolding of a whirling movement whereby the dancer created the material and imaginary space of her performance with 'nothing but the emotion of her dress'.[3] The sole 'emotion' in the dance initially seems to be that of movement for its own sake; and it would be tempting to identify it with the artist's exploration of the specific properties of her medium at the heart of the so-called modernist paradigm. But Mallarmé immediately excludes this idea of modernity. The miracle Loie Fuller offers us is, he says, 'Greek'. It is 'classical in as much as it is utterly modern'.[4] These words are to be taken seriously. What is classical is the union of form and content. Loie Fuller's performance does not express some purely formal quest or sheer virtuosity betraying the status of an avant-garde artist severed from any system of common references. On the contrary, it is the search for a new form of symbolization of the common. The ballerina is a *figurante* – that is, a creator of figures illustrating 'many a spinning image tending towards a distant unfolding'.[5] This is not an artist employing the artifice of a piece of material to generate any movements whatsoever just as she pleases. The

3   Ibid., p. 175.

4   Stéphane Mallarmé, 'Considérations sur l'art du ballet et la Loïe Fuller', *National Observer*, 13 May 1893, in *Oeuvres Complètes*, vol. 2, p. 314.

5   Mallarmé, 'Autre étude de danse', p. 174.

movements she generates with her dress all boil down to a basic model: they are movements of expansion and withdrawal. They symbolize an essence of movement as appearance and disappearance, budding and withdrawing. Here, for Mallarmé, is the very movement whereby natural phenomena become forms of a common sensible world: the rising and setting of the sun, the budding of flowers, the flight of birds, the white foam on the wave. The artifice of art, the artifice with which it invents symbols to express the way humans are in community, is consistent with the movement whereby a world becomes a world. This essence of movement as a form of world was enrolled by traditional ballet in the service of a story to be told and a display of virtuosity. It transformed it into a hierarchical relationship between the star dancer and the anonymous troupe surrounding her. Loie Fuller's dance inverts this inversion and restores the radiating movement of the star to its truth: the expansion through which the artist's self-affirmation is lost in the creation of an impersonal milieu of art.

But nor is the expansion of the movement that creates this impersonal milieu some pantheistic power symbolized by the metaphor of the wave. Dance is not the ecstatic movement that expresses and transmits the energy of universal life. What it constructs and communicates to spectators is images. In fact, grand metaphor is deployed by Mallarmé in a play of metonymies: not the wave but the foam that crowns it; not the flaming setting of the sun but 'delayed decorative leaps of skies, sea, evenings, perfume and foam'.[6] This play of metonymies forms part of a general economy of displacements, analogies and translations: the emotion of a dress, marriage of this 'emotion' with the play of iridescent light, 'transition from sonority to fabrics',[7] translation of a body's gestures into the properties of a space. But this translation itself exists only for a potential translator. The leaps of skies, sea, evenings, perfume and foam delineated by the interaction of fabric and electricity do not exist on the stage. They exist only as the translation of them made by the spectator's reverie. The movement of impersonal life exists only at the price of a double transposition or translation: that of the dancer creating a milieu outside of herself and that of the spectator translating the text (or one of the possible texts) which her movement writes wordlessly.

Dance, then, is not a new art of movement rejecting the old arts of writing and the image in order to chime spontaneously with the rhythm of the bodies and machines creating a new world. What it sets in motion are still images, sentence-images that are combined with other images and translated into other sentences. The marriage between the 'artistic intoxication' of the dress spread out by the dancer and the 'industrial accomplishment' of the coloured projections that make it iridescent seem to furnish an ideal model for fusion between the great symphony of movement and

6 Ibid., p. 176.
7 Ibid., p. 175.

the performance of the dancers. But the promise of fusion is immediately retracted. The performance of the three ecstatic ballerinas is not a manifestation of the new life. It is a way of writing in images, a metaphor that translates the movement of spinning machines or the gestures of telephonists in the telephone exchange before being translated by them in turn. The great symphony of the new life with which art was to fuse remains a scene of metaphors and metonymies where all activities are images that translate one another interminably.

I referred above to the discrepancy between the communism this apotheosis of movement sought to fashion and the communism whose foundations the Soviet government sought to lay. What interests me here is something else: what this dramatization of the movement of dance tells us about dance itself or, more precisely, the paradigm it offers of the dual relationship between thought and the sensible and between art and non-art. The superimposed dance, caught up in a chain of images which translate one another, calls into question the way in which the exemplary character of dance has often been conceived: as the exemplariness of an original encounter between art and life. Earlier, I mentioned two examples of philosophical staging of this 'original encounter'. In Nancy, dance is the original movement whereby a body begins to wrest itself from primitive indistinctness, materialized by the ground on which it rests, like a child in its mother's womb. In Badiou, it is the original intellectual performance of the body that raises itself off the ground to demonstrate its aptitude for receiving ideas. Dance, he says, is not an art. It is the as yet non-artistic manifestation of the body's disposition to art. The 'original encounter' is thus the moment when the body finds itself summoned to its aerial destiny, in accordance with the Platonic definition of man as a 'heavenly plant'. Now, this dramaturgy poses two problems. First of all, it seems to contradict the endeavours of a large number of modern and contemporary dancers and choreographers, who have sought to bring the body back down to earth, to make it display its earthly roots. In Vertov's time, this movement found exemplary expression in the seated position of Mary Wigman, performing her *Witch Dance* (*Hexentanz*) by pressing her knees with her hands to make them knock the ground harder. In the time of Yvonne Rainer and the Judson Dance Theater, this inclination to the ground is expressed as a concern to return dance to the most ordinary acts and tasks of the body in motion: walking, changing direction, shaking one's head, freeing one's arms, leaning, straightening up, handling objects and so on. In another respect, however, the philosophical interpretation of the body that wrests itself from the ground, and the contrary artistic desire to bring dance back down to earth, still have something in common: albeit in opposite ways, they both validate a view of dance as a moment in a primary, solitary relationship between body and ground. This solitude of movement is what Vertov's montage prompts us to query. In the sequence I have analysed, dance is never on its own. The three ballerinas dance superimposed, and their moves are captured in a general movement in which both factory machines and the movements of the crowd in the street, or the ballets of forks and spoons improvised by a member of the workers' club, also participate. It will be said that this is the choice of the director and the process of montage. But that choice is not arbitrary, and montage is not necessarily the obsession of revolutionary filmmakers intent on connecting everything. In its most general form, montage is the practice that puts together things that do not go together, do not seem to go together, or have not as yet been put together. This is the case with the relationship between feet and dress deployed by an American music hall dancer and the inner reverie of a sensitive French poet. It is also the case with the relationship between dance, assembly-line work, everyday activities, and the cinematographic montage that brings them together. Dance symbolizes the translatability of all these movements into one another. In Vertov's film, it is true, this is reduced to a minimum. It is only the formal equivalence of the gestures and the arithmetical equality of quanta of motion. This equivalence nevertheless has to be symbolized. One form of movement must translate the equivalence of all the movements, thereby creating a gap at the heart of the great pantheistic symphony. It is offered to all those who have acted in the course of the day as the very meaning of the community they weave each day with their actions. But it is offered to them as spectators. Obviously, the filmmaker himself attends to presenting their response by showing their amazement at the tricks of montage. This is because, for filmmakers of Vertov's generation, montage was two things at once. It was an original combination of elements, but also faith in the virtue of this assemblage: the expectation that the fragments would be assembled in the spectator's mind in line with the artist's intention and that the energy of the movements would generate a corresponding energy in the viewer.

If dance is in league with montage, it is so in a way that rejects the triple dream of an exact translation of the meaning, an exact translation of the movement, and an equivalence between a way of making sense and a way of setting in motion. Mallarmé reminds us of the discrepancy between the performance of the dance and the spectator's 'translation' of it. Dance is not a movement that creates another movement in those who watch it. It is a particular synthesis of sensible states that summons a different synthesis from the spectator. There is precisely no equivalence. The relation is expressed in the form of a chiasmus: according to Mallarmé, there is the dancer's sensible performance and there is the invisible labour of the spectator's reverie, which strives to 'translate' this performance. This is what is implied by the provocative statement that the dancer does not dance but writes. To this we should add that it is a very particular form of writing. It does not mime any signification. But that does not mean that it is a language peculiar to movement, to be construed as an assemblage of figures pertaining to the vocabulary of ballet, any more than it does to a novel alphabet of movement like the one invented by Rudolf Laban. What transpires between the stage and the audience is neither the communication of a meaning, nor the transmission of a movement. It is precisely an interval. The dancer, wrote Mallarmé once again, moves in space like a 'metaphor encapsulating one of the elementary aspects of our form'.[8] But this metaphor has no translation in any dictionary of tropes. It speaks only from the indeterminacy of what it says. More than any other art, dance might well be the one that expresses the Kantian paradox of purposiveness without any purpose. It is a movement freed from the customary ends of movement designed for some particular goal. But it does not therewith simply contain its own end. It presents itself as *designed for* even though it has no particular design. To say it is a language is, in fact, to say that it is more than a movement: it is a synthesis of sensible states that presents itself as a translation. It is the translation of a text that is still to be written, which the spectator must in a sense re-translate without the aid of a dictionary into a different synthesis of sensible states. Images of movement are going to be integrated into a particular continuum of world experiences, of spectacles glimpsed or dreamed, of images, actions or reveries. Mallarmé speaks in this connection of 'decorative leaps, of skies, sea, evenings, perfume and foam'. This vocabulary

---

8   Stéphane Mallarmé, 'Ballets', *Divagations*, in *Oeuvres Complètes*, vol. 2, p. 171.

from Symbolist times is rather remote from us. But it tells us something that can be expressed in more sober terms, once again borrowed from Kant: dance is, par excellence, an art of *aesthetic ideas*. Aesthetic ideas are those ideas of the imagination that bridge the gap between the conscious ends of art and the aesthetic experience of purposiveness without any purpose. In Kant, it is true, such ideas remain those of the artists, even if they are not themselves conscious of the process of their formation. But what in them was the work of unconscious genius is more aptly regarded as the work of creation of an impersonal sensible environment shared by the wordless writing of dance and the silent translation of the spectator.

I think this twofold movement of translation/transposition is what has given dance its paradigmatic function. The scene of the philosopher witnessing the original movement of dance is a reduction of the more complex dramaturgy of the spectator-poet translating a movement that is itself like the translation of a nonexistent text, a text that is pending. The 'original' scene is secondary to a more original scene, which is precisely not a scene of origin, but one of translation. It is secondary to the analogical set-up at work in the spectacle of the Folies Bergère or on the screen of *Man with a Movie Camera*. Dance performs the role of paradigm via the twofold gap that keeps its gestures doubly at a distance: at a distance from the gestures assigned to useful functions, but also from any fusional choreography of the community. However, this twofold gap has frequently been repressed by modern choreographers, behind either a dramatization of collective energy or a reduction to ordinary gestures. Nevertheless, it regularly resurfaces. So-called postmodern dance has experienced this. The 1960s saw the widespread assertion of a form of dance that wanted Terpsichore shod in sneakers, to distance her not only from the slippers of classical ballet but also from the bare feet of 'expressive dance', and to bring her closer to the essential forms of movement and gestures of the everyday.[9] Twenty years later, many of the dancers and choreographers who had adopted this programme reintroduced forms and sequences of movement derived from the classical vocabulary of dance. This does not, I think, betoken a nostalgic reversion to the past splendours of ballet. Such splendours were not wanting in ballet in sneakers. Rather, the problem was knowing what the sneakers were the translation of, or an analogy for. What has made a comeback is the 'moment of dance', the historical weight of a mode of practice that separates the seeming unity of an original movement from within, so as to introduce into it the gap of a translation – that is, an analogical relationship between two imprints: of movement and of writing.

This is perfectly attested by a piece by Lucinda Childs, whose title – *Dance* – and date (1979) are both emblematic. The work is remarkable not simply for the apotheosis of movement swept up in the crescendo of repetitive figures

9 See Sally Bannes, *Terpsichore in Sneakers: Postmodern Dance* (Middletown, CT: Wesleyan University Press, 1980).

that translate Philip Glass's repetitive music in space. It is even more remarkable for its use of analogy, which seems to be directly inscribed in the dance tradition of Loie Fuller as deciphered by Mallarmé, or Duncan's dance, which Dziga Vertov translated into machine rotations. However, Lucinda Childs went further by making dance its own analogy: the images of female and male dancers were projected onto a transparent screen, in accordance with a montage imagined by Sol LeWitt. The dance was thus performed in two spaces at once: in the real space of the stage and in the imaginary space defined by their enlarged images on the tulle screen. It was performed as its own translation – a translation that amplified its movement only to subtract it from reality, to bring it closer to the spectators' immaterial translation. The enchantments of this new marriage between 'intoxication of art' and 'industrial accomplishment' seem far removed from the minimalism of the pieces that the same Lucinda Childs performed or invented fifteen years earlier. But the duplication of movement that it effects was already present, in more prosaic form, in a piece from 1964 called *Street Dance*, where the dancers in the street had the more modest task of pointing out details of buildings, shop windows or signposts to spectators who were viewing the street from above, with the help of a tape, through the windows of a loft.

The fact is that this process of translation is not confined to sophisticated choreographies. We can find it in the most resolutely minimalist forms of performance. This is true of one of the *Five Dance Constructions* presented in 1961 in New York by Simone Forti, entitled *Platforms*. It presents the most minimal of corporeal performances. A man and a woman slide under wooden boxes placed on the ground. There is thus no longer a single body or body part visible in the area of the action. Parodying the Mallarmé of *A Throw of the Dice*, it might be said that 'nothing will have taken place but the place'. We know, however, that Mallarmé immediately cancelled the hypothesis of this 'nothing' by adding an 'except'. This exceptional supplement, whereby 'one place fuses with the beyond', was a constellation that inscribed the luminous transposition of the number 'on some vacant and superior surface'.[10] In *Platforms*, the supplement to nothing is limited to whistling. From their separate boxes each of the two partners whistles to the other. Thus, the love story and the corporeal performance are reduced to the most basic manifestation of human life and movement: breathing. But the latter suffices to create the space of analogy in the event that the spectators, seated in a circle, associate this distant whistling with some song of love and separation – for example, the 'ancient melody', the melody of the shepherd that Tristan, lying far from Isolde, hears at the start of Act III in Wagner's opera. It will be said that there is a big difference between whistling and an operatic melody played by an English horn. But it is precisely up to spectators to transform the one into the

---

10   Stéphane Mallarmé, 'Un coup de dés jamais n'abolira le hasard', in *Oeuvres Complètes*, vol. 1, p. 387.

equivalent of the other. This role, extending the call of the whistling, is illustrated by a film shot on the occasion of a revival of the piece. At the moment of maximum intensity of the 'love duo', the camera moves away from the two boxes and focuses on the face of a young boy who watches and listens intently, and thus completes the performance without his face telling us *how* he does so. This close-up may remind us of another film devoted to a very different performance: Bergman's *The Magic Flute*, where the overture is filmed through the emotions on a young girl's face. Going back much further, it reminds us of the text where Eisenstein says he had the idea of a 'montage of attractions' by observing during a theatrical rehearsal the face of a child on which all the play's events were reflected.[11] From it he derived the project of an art capable of directly producing the effects reflected by this face, in order to 'plough' the consciousness of spectators. We recognize here the illusion of mastery peculiar to the art of montage: the illusion that confuses the production of a performance with the production of its effect. In fact, reflection on the spectator's face completes the artist's performance only via the milieu of translation/transposition in which it is divested of its mastery.

It will be said that I am commenting on the film of a performance rather than the performance itself. But the camera's lateral movement towards the audience is not a

---

11 Sergei Eisenstein, *Mémoires*, vol. 1, transl. J. Aumont (Paris: UGE, 1978), p. 236.

trick of the filmmaker to enliven an austere spectacle. The very configuration of the performance calls for it. The latter exists only through the space of transpositions and translations that it creates around a sound emitted by two invisible bodies. In its minimalist forms, as in its spectacular forms, dance is an art of displacement and translation. This is what we are reminded of by a performance of a quite different kind, conceived by two French choreographers, Anne Kerzerho and Loïc Touzé. In the performance space, they assemble a number of people who, in their various ways, employ a certain bodily dexterity when performing their daily work. But, if they are assembled, it is no longer, as in the 1960s, to compose a choreography drawn from the gestures of work or everyday life. It is to sit down at tables and talk. It is to translate their adept gestures into a narrative for others and to listen to the narrative in which others translate their own know-how. This exchange of translations might remind us of the principle of intellectual emancipation formulated nearly two centuries ago by Joseph Jacotot: an emancipated man or woman is a person capable of speaking about the activity they perform, capable of conceiving this activity as a form of language. We should be clear about what this 'language' means. It is not a system of signs, but a power of address that aims to weave a certain form of community: a community of beings who share the same sensible world in as much as they remain distant from one another and create figures to communicate across distance while maintaining this distance. An emancipated community, Jacotot said, is a community of narrators and translators. It is perhaps in this unexpected sense that dance is (as Mallarmé put it) an emblematic art or an emblem of art.

4

CINEMATIC MOMENTS

The title of this chapter is to be understood in several senses. In the first instance, the moments in question are three extracts from films on which I wish to comment. The three films they are taken from also correspond to three different moments in the history of cinema: the experimental moment of the 1920s; the classical moment of Hollywood, represented by a film dating from 1940; and the contemporary moment illustrated by a film from the beginning of the century. But I have also selected these moments from films deriving from different moments in the history of cinema, because these films speak to us of their time, as ordinarily understood. They speak to us of the historical moment when they were conceived and made; they variously bear witness to the conflicts, hopes and disillusionment that marked the history of the twentieth century. Finally – and this is the most important aspect – in order to speak to us of their time, the directors of these films adopted a certain treatment of cinematic time. Reflecting on these cinematic moments will therefore involve working on the complex relationship between several temporalities: between the modes of structuration of time at work in the sequence of images in films, changes in those modes in the history of cinema, and their relations with the more general history that they seek to express. I would like to show how cinema, in order to think and express the history it pertains to, has utilized its most essential resource: its capacity to put several times in a single time – that is, several modes of temporality in a determinate temporal sequence. The three moments selected thus present various combinations of different modes of temporal articulation: between continuity and fragmentation, sequence and repetition, succession and coexistence. But they are also so many ways of grasping the time of History understood as collective destiny. I shall try to show how they do so in a state of tension between several temporalities: a temporality of narrative, a temporality of performance, and a temporality of myth. These notions will be clarified as and when I analyse the relevant moments. For now, I shall make do with a very general definition of them. The temporality of narrative presents itself as corresponding to a lived temporality; the temporality of performance, by contrast, is a constructed, autonomous temporality; and the temporality of myth is what brings an instance of the extra-temporal into play in narrative.

I shall start with one of the most significant films of the 1920s – that is, the moment of conjunction between experimentation in the new medium of cinema and the great social experiment called revolution – the same film with which I have already sought to re-define what the notion of modernity might mean, and the role played in it by dance: Dziga Vertov's *Man with a Movie Camera*. In it, the filmmaker makes a radical decision as regards the use of time. He makes a film without a narrated story and without actors playing characters. In their stead, he offers 'an experiment in the cinematic communication of actual facts'. To communicate is to do the work of language. But this language is not a mere medium for exhibiting a reality supposedly external to it. If it were, the use of filmic time would not be different from that of the narrated story. It is an experimental language. Its words do not speak reality. They are themselves realities, gestures taken from everyday life and work. Hence cinematic communication is not a way of talking about the reality of the communism being constructed in the Soviet Union. It is a way of constructing it. To communicate is not to transmit information, but to link activities. Cinematic language constructs the sensible reality of communism by linking a multiplicity of movements. By assembling, in a single totality, the movements of a multitude of bodies in motion, of working hands or of cogs in machines, cinema creates the sensible fabric of the new life. The new language is therefore not simply a language of images; and montage is not simply the art of connecting images that Godard refers to in his *Histoire(s) du cinéma*. It is a way of connecting times, of putting a multiplicity of uses of time and modes of temporality in one and the same temporal sequence.

This construction is effected by Vertov within an empirical temporal unit: the day. The film's setting is an ordinary day, from waking in the morning through the working day to the evening's entertainment. We might wish to associate this form, employed by several of the filmmakers of the time, to the genre of documentary. But the story of a day is not the documentation of a day. It is a fictional structure characteristic of the age, which is illustrated by two literary works that can scarcely be assigned to the genre of documentary reportage: Joyce's *Ulysses* and Woolf's *Mrs Dalloway*. But it is also a fictional structure that corresponds to a revolution in fiction. Explicitly or implicitly, fictional logic had hitherto been governed by the Aristotelian distinction between two types of temporality: on the one hand, the time of the chronicle that describes things as they happen, one after another; on the other, the time of fictional rationality, which shows us how things *might happen*. In it the order of the unfolding of time is identified with the development of a causal logic. This distinction between two types of temporality was itself based on the contrast between two forms of use of time and two forms of life: on one side, the time of so-called passive men inhabiting the everyday universe of things happening one after another; on the other, the time of so-called active men living the time of projected ends and means that potentially generate effects other than those projected. By contrast, the new fiction invokes the time of the everyday, comprising a multiplicity of microscopic sensible events, all equally important, which link the life of each individual to anonymous life in general, which knows no hierarchy. That is why the setting of the day does not simply substitute the empirical succession of minor facts for the causal sequence of great events. More profoundly, it replaces the time of succession – a hierarchical time – with an egalitarian time of coexistence.

This fictional democracy is what Vertov's montage of the day seeks to transform into a construction of communist time. The activities assembled by montage are not a chronicle following the course of the hours. They are so many body and machine movements, so many hand gestures, which are to be linked by making them synchronic through two basic operations: fragmenting them into very short sequences, units of movements detached from their specific purpose; and merging them into one another very rapidly, so as to sweep them up in a single general rhythm. This dual operation is particularly marked in the section I would like to comment on, which comes midway through the film, between two episodes presenting a continuous action: first an ambulance and a vehicle with firemen going to the aid of victims; then the movement of a platform from which the cameraman is filming a hydroelectric station. Between these two moments comes an episode of around four minutes that comprises a montage of the most diverse activities: the ministrations of a beautician or shoe-shiner, the sharpening of an axe or barber's razor, the gestures of a hand that sews or operates a sewing machine, those of an assembly-line worker making cigarette packets, typists in a typing pool, operators in a telephone exchange, and many others, including those of the cameraman who turns his handle and the editor who cuts, scrapes and glues the film.

What confers unity on this temporal sequence, which displays separate, heterogeneous activities concurrently, is the very rhythm of its fragmentation: almost 120 shots in a little under four minutes. The only camera movement throughout this part seems to denounce its own inadequacy by circulating extremely rapidly between two female workers, as if to show *a contrario* that the montage of separate fragments is much better suited to expressing movement. A little later, in the Lenin Club sequence, the film reaches the speed of thirty-five shots in twenty-five seconds, not counting double exposures. The radical use of fragmentation here calls for a remark about the meaning of this procedure. Fragmentation has been equated by some with the loss of experience constitutive of modernity, and by others with an authoritarian construction of the relationship between images and meanings, corresponding, in the world of art, to the model of the Taylorist division of labour. Neither of these conceptions applies in this instance. Fragmentation is not a form of separation signalling a loss of meaning. On the contrary, it is the formation of a new common sense. And it is quite the reverse of a Taylorist division of labour. The latter breaks a task up into several complementary operations. By contrast, Vertov's montage erases all differences, and is not concerned with complementarity. It does not bother showing us where the packets casually thrown over her shoulder by the female worker in the cigarette factory land. It makes all the activities identical units of movement, merging them into the same sensible continuum. To that end, it separates them both from the temporality defined by their own ends and from the hierarchy of the forms of life to which they pertain. That is why the actions of the manicurist doing the nails of a customer of bourgeois appearance, of the assembly-line workers in a cigarette factory, of the street shoe-shiner, and of the employees in a telephone exchange are rendered equivalent, even though some pertain to the old bourgeois world and others to the new industrial, socialist world. All these operations are hand gestures rendered equivalent by fragmentation and acceleration. What is communist is not the nature of the activities, but the nature of their connection, their capacity to merge with one another as equivalent elements in one overall movement. Fragmentation is not a way of separating. On the contrary, it is a way of uniting.

This is how the film seeks to respond to the task assigned to it by the time it inhabits: it perceptibly constructs the common time of the new life through a use of cinematic time that homogenizes all activities and makes them merge with one another. This form of time is opposed to the traditional time of the sequences of fiction. It remains to be seen what type of temporality the unity thus constructed belongs to. Now, there is a privileged form of temporality that aesthetic modernity has made the antithesis of the old logic of stories: that of performance. Performance is the movement that unfolds, and folds back on itself, in a series of metamorphoses. In this sense, the cinematic construction of the Soviet day is the construction of a performance. That is why Vertov pointedly includes a very specific activity in this day: that of the conjuror, creator of metamorphoses that enchant children. Above all, this is why the symphony of the day is framed within another time: that of the cinematic spectacle. The film begins in a cinema, where the seats lower automatically to receive visitors and where a conductor's baton gives the signal for the visual symphony to come. At the end of the film, we return to this cinema, where we see the spectators watch their day transformed into a collective performance. These spectators are, in fact, the 'actors' in the film: those whose bodies in motion, dextrous gestures and joyful expressions have been assembled in the great symphony. The film screening in which they are the spectators is, in fact, a means of reducing the multiplicity of the moments of this symphony to a few symbols of common movement: the gestures of the telephonists constantly making new connections, the smile of a female worker superimposed on the movement of the spinning wheel, but also the gestures of a female conductor, of trumpets whose images merge in the same visual vertigo, of dancers whose movements convey the élan of the collective symphony, and first of all a camera that comes out of its box to greet the audience, before returning to its box. The great unanimous symphony of communist life is pitted against the time of old sentimental stories only by ultimately being identified with the time of pure performance, which unfolds itself before withdrawing into itself.

This identification of the new Soviet life with its happy symphony of equal movements has prompted many criticisms. I shall dwell on only one of them – more precisely, on a film which the following year offered a de facto critique of Vertov's film, especially its use of time. The film is Eisenstein's *The General Line*, whose original title, *The Old and the New*, clearly contrasts two times and two forms of life. In it, Eisenstein teaches his colleague Vertov that there is no happy symphony encompassing treatment in a beauty parlour and assembly-line work in the same rhythm. There is a rhythm of the old world and a rhythm of the new world. But the difference between the two is not to be found where one might think. What differentiates the new from the old is not the fact that it is synchronic and that it proceeds more quickly. The old is not so much the old methods of culture, like the ceremonies of priests to make it rain, as the delirium of prostration and genuflection in which the people abase themselves. The new consists not only in machines as perfect automata. The tractor begins by breaking down, and its repair requires the peasant Marfa to sacrifice her skirt and her modesty. Machines are objects of love and sacrifice. Thus, the famous cream separator is transformed into an object of Eucharistic adoration. The new time, according to Eisenstein, is not that of the conjuring tricks beloved of Vertov. It is the time of the great orgiastic feasts encapsulated in his film by the bull's breeding ritual or the overflowing streams of milk: a Dionysiac trance whose exaltation is contrasted with the movement that bends the believers' bodies earthwards. The language of cinema is not the performance that unfolds and folds up again, but a primitive language that makes the utter novelty of history communicate in step with the immemorial time of myth. In complete contrast to Vertov, the montage practised by Eisenstein is a desynchronization of times.

This desynchronization is still operative, in a different way, at the heart of classical Hollywood cinema, the dream factory in a darkened room that Godard compares to the Soviet dream factory. I would like to show this in connection with a film that seemingly obeys a traditional narrative logic. In fact, its screenplay is taken from a successful novel dealing with a major contemporary social problem, and the story is structured around a main character played by a star actor. This film is *The Grapes of Wrath*, made in 1940 by John Ford and based on John Steinbeck's novel, which relates the exodus of the Oklahoma farmers, driven from their land by the twofold impact of the dust bowl and mechanization, and then confronted in California by the savage exploitation of farmhands by the capitalist trusts of the fruit industry. The straight line of this story is split in two from the outset by a different temporality, which we find at work in an episode at the start of the film in the house where the son coming out of prison – Tom Joad – arrives to look for his parents, accompanied by the defrocked pastor Casy. Instead of his family, Tom finds an abandoned house where an erratic character is hiding out – the sharecropper Muley, who will recount to him the expropriation of which his own family and all sharecroppers are the victims.

The long sequence of Muley's narrative centres on two powerful images: first of all the army of caterpillars that seem like mythological monsters; and then the arrival of a character on whom the low-angle shot confers a colossal dimension, the tractor driver in leather gaiters and pilot's goggles who will demolish Muley's house before continuing calmly on his way. We recognize these images straight away. They seem to be a replica of the army of machines and the hero of new times celebrated in *The General Line*: the proud tractor driver who smashed the barriers of the individual properties as he advanced and secured victory over the kulaks for the *kolkhoz*. Here, the driver of the caterpillar still represents the embodiment of a new time, but the image has changed sides. The proud tractor driver is the agent of the anonymous power of finance which, to drive the peasants from their land, goes as far as razing their homes. We could comment at length on this inversion, which transforms the emblem of emancipation, bound up

John Ford, *The Grapes of Wrath*, 1940.

with the time of progress, into an emblem of oppression. In the same year, an author far removed from Hollywood, Walter Benjamin, wrote his *Theses on the Philosophy of History*, which denounced the 'pile of debris' of progress. But what interests me here is the type of temporality within which this inversion of symbols occurs, and the relationship it implies between the story told by the film and the History to which it bears witness. At this point, in fact, the film introduces a significant condensation compared with the novel.

The latter concisely describes, in one chapter, the way the expulsions occurred. In the film, the story is seen from the perspective of a character, the above-mentioned

Sergei Eisenstein, *The General Line*, 1929.

Muley. The character himself seems to have emerged from nothingness in a house plunged into darkness, where the flame of a candle transforms the characters into ghostly apparitions. A slight noise guides Tom Joad and his candle towards the corner where Muley is hiding and reveals his distraught face, which seems utterly haunted by what he has lived through. The story is first conveyed by him in a declamation reminiscent of Shakespeare. Then a play of fade-outs, which seems to follow the direction of his gaze, connects the present of this dialogue of shadows and the narrative of the moments of the expulsion, as if we were seeing not simply what Muley says, but what has been imprinted on his retina at that moment. The expulsion of the farmers, which gives the story its motor, thus exists only in the distraught gaze and speech of the ghostlike

John Ford, *The Grapes of Wrath*, 1940.

character whose nightmare it is – a character whose performance steers the film sequence for these seven or eight minutes, before disappearing from the story.

It is as if, with his momentary performance, the relationship between story and History splits in two. The expulsion is the event that will set the Joad tribe and the former pastor on the road to California. But this event will only have existed visually as the nightmare or trauma of an individual who, for his part, will not leave: the man struck by injustice, whose fate condenses that of all those whom the same violence has affected and who, for that very reason, are removed from the narrative combinations of stories stretching towards their conclusions. In a sense, these eight minutes, which mark the passage of History – in this instance, capitalism – over the configuration of a region, are like a moment detached from the plot, assigned to a supporting actor who in those eight minutes will make his own film. But this supporting actor, John Qualen, is not just anyone. He symbolizes a moment in American history and legend. Norwegian by birth, Qualen spent thirty years in Hollywood films frequently playing the same role: that of the Scandinavian immigrant attached to the land vouchsafed by the American New World. Seven years earlier, he had acted in King Vidor's *Our Daily Bread*, a work emblematic of the great expectations of the Roosevelt era, glorifying a fraternal agricultural community that offered a new life to those driven from the towns by the economic crisis. The film's high point is the collective endeavour to dig the canal that will make it possible to irrigate the land. In the tension on the faces waiting for the water to gush, and the enthusiasm aroused by its surge, we have something like an American transposition of Russian scenarios of the victorious *kolkhoz*. Now, it is this scenario – or, if you like, this conjunction of scenarios – whose end the same actor seems to embody. His singular performance as a distraught man connects the wound of History to a time now separated from any future; it connects it to the extra-temporality of myth. But myth here no longer signifies, as it does in Eisenstein, primitive language, the language of symbols that separates itself from the narrative action only to intensify and magnify the driving of the tractors of the new life. Muley's distraught vision, by inverting the glorious scene of the hero of new times, makes the mythical element not what celebrates the forward march of history, but what divides it irredeemably.

Here, we might compare Muley's story with Brecht's scripts, which in the same era opposed the dialectic of history to those who suffer it passively. *The Grapes of Wrath* is contemporaneous with *Mother Courage*, the story of a woman who persists in not understanding the war waged on human beings by the logic of profit. In the 1950s, Barthes summarized the play's effect in a famous formula: 'because we see Mother Courage blind, we see what she does not see'.[1] A different dialectic is offered to us by

---

1   Roland Barthes, 'Mère Courage aveugle', in *Écrits sur la théâtre*, ed. Jean-Loup Rivière (Paris: Editions du Seuil, 2002), p. 184.

the division of time in Ford's film. The extra-temporality
in which Muley is sunk is not the night of ignorance and
passivity, as opposed to the broad daylight of struggle and
awareness. It is the time of an inscription of the irreparable.
This time seems to revoke any story of salvation. But it is
also what gives these stories their radicalism, the stamp of
the irreconcilable. This separate moment divides the line
of the narrated story in two. On the one hand, the story
of Tom Joad is one of a peasant driven from his land who
goes off to discover, thanks to his condition as agrarian
worker, the reality of class struggle and the consciousness of a fighting labourer. But this path from obscurity
to clarity is doubled by a story of shadows that flit from
night to night, from semi-darkness to semi-darkness, from
hallucination to hallucination. It is in the night, in a tent
lit by candlelight, that Tom will find the former preacher
Casy, who has become a union leader and who will soon
be killed by the bosses' henchmen. And it is in the night
that, threatened in turn, he will say farewell to his mother,
maintaining that he will henceforth be present in invisible
fashion wherever men and women fight for their dignity.
Originally, the film was to end with Tom's departure. The
end finally chosen – the optimistic ending where, in the
lorry taking what remains of the family, Tom's mother
affirms her faith in the indestructible power of the people –
was insisted on by the producer Darryl Zanuck. The logic
of the film shot by Ford transformed the fighter for the
people's future into an invisible presence, a shadow sunk

in the same night from which Muley had emerged for a moment at the beginning, before disappearing forever. The movement from night to night, and from semi-darkness to semi-darkness, does not erase the violence of the testimony on the ferocity of social exploitation. On the contrary, that violence is radicalized by the mythical dimension imparted to the exodus of the deprived peasants by these three distraught bodies. The film narrates the class struggle in two ways: on the Aristotelian model of the transition from ignorance to knowledge, but also as the repetition of a hallucinated series of patches of light in the dark. It narrates it in the discrepancy between two temporalities that occupy the same time. And it is through this split that it bears witness to History – that is to say, what capitalism does to human beings.

The balance of a story that is seemingly linear, but in fact informed by gaps, stasis and hidden vertigo, might define the classical age of cinema, in contrast to the symbolic age – which Vertov's film could be taken to embody – when the cinema claimed to construct the reality of a new sensible world with its own resources. In the Hegelian tradition, the classical moment is the one in which the form and content of art correspond to one another. The classical moment of cinema would then be the one where it is capable of integrating into the continuity of the movement of images the temporal gaps or vertigo that contradict it. It would express a historical moment when the balance of forces in a society is clearly visible and interpretable. With this classicism, it would be tempting, in Hegelian terms, to contrast the Romantic moment, when content and form separate again, or – in a more contemporary framework – the postmodern moment, when any possible narratives about society and history have been wrecked in the great disasters of the history of a century and the collapse of grand narratives. However, it seems to me that this grand schema cannot account for the interlacing of temporalities at work in the forms that attempt most acutely to account for our present.

I would like to show this with a sequence in a film that reformulates the old Aristotelian problem of the relations between the time of chronicle and the time of fiction. *Juventude em marcha* ('Forward youth', entitled *Colossal Youth* in English) belongs to the series of films – four to date – that Pedro Costa has devoted to the life of a small number of immigrants from Cape Verde and other outsiders in the suburbs of Lisbon. These films seem to attest to a sort of endgame – the endpoint of a trajectory in which Vertov's symphony would represent the starting-point, and class struggle à la John Ford the median point. In effect, it shows us workers without work and without a working class, without class struggle and with no expectation of any future. To the existence of workers who are orphans of any class struggle, there seems to correspond the time without the history of the chronicle – the time counterposed by Aristotle to the rationality of tragic fiction or which, more recently, Althusser contrasted with the dialectical

rationality of theatre. It is precisely the time of the chronicle that seems to be followed by Pedro Costa's protracted
inquiry into a shanty town in the process of being demol-
ished, and then the white cubes where its inhabitants have
been rehoused. Such immersion in the everyday seemed to
be symbolized by the title of his previous film *In Vanda's
Room*, the product of two years spent in the room where
Vanda, her sister and her friends endlessly discussed their
life between two sessions preparing cocaine. It might
seem as if *Juventude em marcha* likewise synchronizes its
slow pace with the slowed-down time of his characters
– especially his main character, the Cape Verdean brick-
layer Ventura. What we see are various minor scenes from
daily life: stories about work and accidents at work, card
games with his colleague Lento, meetings with the council
employee to obtain a council flat in the name of a ficti-
tious family, various visits and conversations. These scenes
seem too banal, too rooted in the everyday, to be anything
other than documentation. Very soon, however, the way
they succeed one another without any connection under-
mines our faith in the documentary character of what we
are watching. An episode presented in an indistinct present
seems to be a reminiscence of a remote time. On another
occasion, we see Ventura set off for work with Lento, only
to find him in the next episode alone in a black suit between
two paintings at the Gulbenkian Foundation. It is on one of
these breaks in the temporal continuum that I would like to
comment, focusing on an episode near the end of the film.

Pedro Costa, *Colossal Youth*, 2006.

The start of this sequence effects a consummate shift between two spaces and two times. At the outset, Ventura is in the wretched street of a shanty town, just emerging from one of his visits. We next see him enter a hall typical of recent but already deteriorating social housing for another visit. He knocks on a door whose brown-coloured blisters invade the screen in close-up. This close-up introduces a break between spaces and times. On the other side of the door, we are no longer in the same temporality. The rupture is marked by the ceremonious character of the gestures made by the person who receives Ventura in an empty flat whose walls are blackened by smoke, his colleague Lento. Throughout the film, Lento has contrasted

his massive, obtuse silhouette with the black silhouette, at
once wild and elegant, of Ventura. Next to Ventura, Lento
has embodied the figure of the coarse, illiterate worker to
whom he vainly sought to teach the text of a love letter
intended for his beloved in Cape Verde. Lento now dis-
cards the cover of the burly, stupid worker. He becomes
a seer emerging from the night, similar to the enlightened
Muley. He takes the hand held out to him by Ventura, and
both stand before us in a posture unusual in cinema. They
are like stage actors, and their dialogue assumes the rhythm
of a tragic psalmody with its alternate voices. Later, Lento
will proudly recite the famous love letter he had always
been incapable of memorizing. In the interim, in the same
ceremonious tone, he will have recounted how he lost his
wife and children in the fire he himself started in despair at
his condition. And he will have shown his hands to testify
to the marks of the fire. 'All burnt', says Ventura. The
hands we see, however, show no signs of burning. This
visual discrepancy is slight compared with the narrative
gap imposed on the film's spectators by this scene. For the
Lento they had seen hitherto had neither wife nor child.
And, above all, they had already seen him die, falling from
the electricity pole to which he was trying to connect the
shack he shared with Ventura. The impossibility of linking
this episode with the others in a narrative continuum
requires the audience to understand what the seemingly
nonchalant pace of the narrative has hitherto concealed:
the film's episodes are not lived moments in the existence

of two immigrants caught on camera. They are fictions, but fictions of a particular kind: not stories of fictional characters played by actors, but minor scenes in the manner of Brecht's *Fear and Misery of the Third Reich*: scenes that are forms of condensation of their story and those of all migrant workers who share their fate in the metropolises of Capital. What Lento narrates did not happen to him. But it did happen to a family of immigrants from Cape Verde during the shooting of the film. And their story has been integrated into the performance given by Ventura and Lento. They simply do not give it as actors assuming roles. They do it with their bodies scarred by exile and exploitation, bodies that carry the general scar of the condition they speak of, even if what they say happened to others. The same applies to Pedro Costa's real workers as to John Ford's fictional farmer. Their performance bears witness to History – that is, in this instance, to what colonization and immigration have done to human beings – in as much as it is situated in a kind of extra-temporality. The twice-dead Lento whom we see is something like one of the living dead, an inhabitant of Hell who has returned to our world to bear witness to the hells present at the heart of it. As an inhabitant of Hell, he can make the life of all those who share his condition appear for what it is: a life suspended between life and death, a life of the living dead. With a voice that speaks from beyond life, he can judge the trajectory of Ventura, who has finally obtained his identity card, social security and social housing, but is nonetheless alone with the wounds inflicted on him by exploitation. The time of the performance is thus tied up with the time of myth to narrate the passage of History – that is, colonialism and capitalism – over bodies. And this interlacing of times shatters the consensual framework within which our societies perceive Ventura, Lento and their fellows. It doubly shifts the place allotted to the migrant worker by the dominant regime of the visible and the sayable. On the one hand, poor migrants are more than poor migrants: they are artists, capable of transforming their story into so many little sketches of which they become the interpreters. On the other, they are less than migrant workers: they are so many living-dead, inhabitants of Hell. But this living-dead identity is itself dual. On one side, Lento and Ventura are mutant bodies, like the zombies, leopard men or cat women represented by a filmmaker contemporaneous with John Ford, Jacques Tourneur, who is a particular favourite of Pedro Costa. On the other, they are judges from Hell come to judge the living.

Thus, like the great exodus of farmers driven from their land, the seemingly familiar chronicle of the life of migrants in the suburbs of Lisbon opens out into a radical disjunction of times. But classical film narrative was able to integrate discordant time, the mark of the irreparable, as a scarcely perceptible division in the unfolding of the narrative. This is what the story of the errant migrants seems no longer to permit. The extra-temporality of the irreparable and of myth is now introduced into the heart of the chronicle. The time of exploitation to which they doubly attest, as actors and as bodies that are bearers of history, prohibits the film from unfolding as a sequence of events progressing from a beginning to an end. Correspondingly, it rules out any reparation for the violence they have suffered from a history marching towards a future. The court of Hell sketched here by Pedro Costa will be given substance in his next film, *Cavalo Dinheiro*, which puts on trial the last great promise of collective emancipation – namely, the Portuguese Carnation Revolution whose shadow side for Pedro Costa is represented by the story of Ventura and his colleagues. There is no longer any time of historical development that might accompany the time of the film's episodes and hold out the promise of a future justice for the injustice which these voices tell of and these bodies display. Justice is shown as extra-temporal, as something that can only come from a radical outside relative to the time of progress, which is merely the time of the progress of exploitation.

These three films involve very different temporal configurations. However, each is shot through by an internal rupture; and all three signal a distance from the progressivist model made dominant by the Marxist tradition, which has often served as a criterion for judging the politics of art: the model wherein History functions both as an instance of truth that justifies the linkages of fiction and as a promise of justice for the conflicts it exhibits. The communist Vertov dramatizes a time of generalized simultaneity where the class struggle no longer has a place, supplanted as it has been by the unanimous symphony of movement. Under the sign of art-become-life, he proposes a time whose model is, in reality, that of artistic performance. We might ironically apply to his film the sentence in which Marx encapsulated Proudhon's position: 'There has been history, but there is no longer any.' For his part, Ford represents the persistence of class struggle, but also its distance from the progressivist scenario of an advancing history. He doubles a narrative plot of struggle and achievement of awareness with a singular performance linking the time of History to the extra-temporality of myth. The irony here is that it is the man of Capital, the film's producer, who sews up the tear and ends the film with a victory for the people, meeting the commercial requirement for a happy ending. In Pedro Costa, the relationship between the time of performance and that of myth seems to have completely devoured the instance of narrative, asserting that it alone is capable today of conveying the violence of exploitation and the violence of rejection. The film exhibits a radical split between the scenario of justice and the time of progress, be it historical progress or the progression of the narrative. This split opens out into a much larger problem, which is thinking the temporality of politics today. I shall limit myself here to what concerns the temporality of the film and its relationship with its time, which attests to a third form of irony. The time made for some of the exploited to say what domination has done to them is a time that the film industry declares incompatible with that of cinemas, and tends to exile to the extra-temporality of museums.

INDEX